bedding
plants

JimHole LoisHole

questions/**ANSWERS**

volume 1

bedding
plants

Practical Advice and the
Science Behind It

H
HOLE'S

ENJOY GARDENING

PUBLISHED BY HOLE'S
   101 Bellerose Drive
   St. Albert, Alberta Canada
   T8N 8N8

Printed in Canada   5   4   3   2   1

Canadian Cataloguing in Publication Data

Hole, Lois, 1933-
   Bedding plants

   (Questions & answers ; 1)
   Includes index.
   ISBN 0-9682791-5-5

   1. Annuals (Plants) 2. Flower gardening. I. Hole, Jim, 1956- II.
Title. III. Series: Questions & answers (St. Albert, Alta.) ; 1.
SB423.75.C3H64 2000   635.9'312   C00-910316-3

Printed and bound by Friesens, Altona, Manitoba, Canada

Contents

Acknowledgements

For being there with the answers when we had questions, special thanks to Valerie Hole and Dave Grice.

We also wish to extend a very special thanks to our staff members, who diligently recorded hundreds of gardening questions (and answers) from our customers during the always-hectic spring rush.

And of course, we'd like to thank all those customers, and everyone who ever came out to hear us speak—this book is as much theirs as it is ours!

The *Q&A* Series—
Practical Advice
and the Science Behind It

Success is built on a solid foundation of questions. Every innovation comes
about because someone asked, "how does this process work? And how can I
make it work better?" A good question can open up whole new worlds—
new ways of doing things, new perspectives, and new information about
secrets once hidden.

That information is what good gardening is all about. Our goal has always
been to provide gardeners, no matter what their skill level, with the information they need to grow beautiful plants—and to accomplish this in the
most enjoyable manner. Accordingly, different people want different kinds of
information. We've answered the questions in these books in two parts: a
short answer for those who are eager to solve a problem and get back to
their projects, and a more in-depth answer for those who want to spend a
little time to learn the deeper issues of their favourite hobby. In short, we
deliver practical advice and the science behind it.

At Hole's, we've always tried to ask the right questions and to listen carefully
when they come from someone else. The questions in the *Q&A* books
didn't spring from our heads—they were collected from hundreds of people,
from coast to coast. Over the past dozen years, we've been recording the
best questions we've run across, from the simple questions we thought
beginning gardeners could identify with to the head-scratchers that gave us
pause. The inquiries came from walk-in customers, letters, phone calls, and
e-mails. Some came from audiences during one or another of our radio or
television appearances; others from the folks we've spoken to at gardening
talks all across the continent. A few came from our own employees during
the day-to-day operations of our greenhouse. No matter what the source,
each inquiry contained within itself a valuable piece of information: it told
us what people wanted to know and gave us a guide with which to build
this series of books.

Answering these questions has been as valuable for us as for the questioners;
they've pushed us to the limits of our knowledge, urging us to dig deeper
for the truth.

Lois Hole and Jim Hole
March, 2000

Introduction
by Lois Hole

Over the years, my son Jim and I have learned a lot about annuals, but not without a good deal of trial and error and more than a few minor catastrophes. Through it all, we've used a combination of our own experiences and knowledge gleaned from books, courses, and our neighbours, customers, and fellow growers to gradually improve the way we garden. To raise bedding plants—or any plants, for that matter—to their full potential, there's really only one quality a good gardener needs: a willingness to learn and adapt.

The First Greenhouse

That willingness certainly came in handy when my husband Ted first suggested we set up a greenhouse on our northern Alberta vegetable farm. At first, I wasn't in favour of the idea, to put it mildly; I thought the greenhouse would interfere with our market-gardening business. "Don't worry, Lois, we'll just use it to grow some extra vegetables," Ted assured me. So, I reluctantly agreed and soon enough our first greenhouse, made of wooden planks and sheets of construction-grade plastic, sprang up beside the garage. It was only 2,500 square feet, but it worked well enough for our purposes, and I started to think that the new facility might come in handy for the vegetable business after all.

Of course, the first question that people asked me when they saw the greenhouse was "why don't you have any flowers?"

That was 1965, and we've been growing bedding plants ever since—although now in 120,000 square feet of space rather than 2,500!

Ted's Approach

Ted started the scientific yet practical approach to running the farm and greenhouse. A graduate of the University of Alberta, Ted was completely willing to use all the resources at his command to make the greenhouse business a success. His studies made him aware of the fact that water high in soda (commonly called sodium)—like the water in our well—was inappropriate to use on plants, so we avoided a potentially costly mistake.

In that case, Ted's store of knowledge was sufficient. But when the tomatoes in our first greenhouse began to wilt and die inexplicably, Ted needed to turn to the experts for help. He took a few specimens of the tomato foliage down to Alberta Agriculture and had them analyzed. "There's definitely a toxin present in these plants," Ted was told, "and it looks like a wood preservative." It didn't take long to deduce that the treated support poles we'd used in the greenhouse were the culprits. (Many construction timbers are treated with chemicals to forestall rotting. Great for the timbers, but not so great for nearby plants!) Once we gave the poles several layers of enamel paint to block the fumes, the problem was solved.

Mr. Science

Our younger son, Jim, inherited much of this investigative spirit from his father. Jim was studious and tended to gravitate to the farm chores that allowed him to investigate the mysteries of nature. Jim could often be found observing bugs, working with chemicals, and poking at the dirt with his fingers to see if he could find some germinating seeds. He also kept the farm vehicles in working order and remains a car buff to this day.

Jim's interest in chemistry and biology served us well on many occasions, especially when he began his studies at the University of Alberta, where he absorbed a truckload of academic information to add to his field experience. At one point, we were having trouble getting cauliflower transplants to grow. The plants would get to a certain size, then stop. Jim, armed with his new knowledge, pointed out that we were leaving cauliflower seedlings in the packs too long and the roots were getting cramped. "It's called buttoning," Jim explained. "If you don't give the roots room to grow, the plant responds by initiating flowering, which arrests its growth. That's why they don't grow anymore, even after you give the roots more space." It wasn't too long after this that Valerie, Jim's sister-in-law, started calling Jim "Mr. Science," and soon enough others picked up on the nickname. (Even today, Jim typically responds to it with a theatrical bit of eye-rolling.)

Jim Hole at the EuroGro '99 Conference, Warwick, England.

Jim's expertise grew until "ask Jim!" became a common phrase at the greenhouse. I used it quite a few times myself when I started doing gardening talks across the country. I was pretty good at fielding most questions, but from time to time someone gave me a stumper like, "what's the life cycle of the Asian long-horned beetle?" "Ask Jim!" I would shout across the audience—and then I'd give out his phone number, much to his chagrin. Jim's strength lies not so much in encyclopedic knowledge, but in his willingness to ferret out information from a variety of sources: his books, other growers, and a variety of experts working in labs and universities in Canada, Europe, and the United States.

I've come to rely on Jim's skills more and more as the years have passed. The truth is, I was fine when I only had to deal with a few dozen plants. But when you're talking about 30,000 different varieties, it's time to delegate. Indeed, the knowledge at our greenhouse is carried around in over a dozen different heads. Jim and I depend on all of them to provide advice on everything from the best remedy for blackspot on roses to how to plant a shade tree properly.

The Experienced Eye

Naturally, experience plays a large role in gardening, too. After you've been growing plants for a while, you start to develop an instinct for when things are going wrong. I remember one early-spring evening when Ted and I were heading out to Edmonton to see a movie. As we were heading to the car, I noticed that the frost had crept higher up the sides of one of the greenhouses than it usually does. The difference wasn't large, but it set off alarm bells in my head anyway, and sure enough, when we checked out the greenhouse, a heater had failed. A simple enough problem to correct when caught early, but one that took some experience to notice.

Sometimes experience just means repeating what works, even if you don't immediately understand why a particular strategy paid off. I had huge problems getting the seed of Blue Himalayan poppies to germinate before I carelessly left them on a cold cement floor. Up came the seedlings after just a few days! It wasn't until much later that we learned that Blue Himalayan poppy seeds need to go through a cold period, called stratification, before they will germinate.

The Best Combination

On the other hand, simply repeating what works without understanding the science behind it can backfire. A seasoned greenhouse operator we knew, Clarence Gamber, grew excellent petunias for retail sales. "People should plant annuals when they're still green in the packs, but people never buy them that way, so you may as well time things so that the petunias are in full bloom in May," Clarence would say, and he was quite right. One year, he managed to get a crop to bloom at just the right time, and his petunias sold like hotcakes. But when he tripled his stock the following year, he missed his blooming timing entirely and sold far fewer plants. "That's where the science comes in," Jim recalled when I discussed this story with him. "Clarence tried to repeat the conditions that led to his initial success, but he didn't take into account all of the environmental and physiological factors. Getting a petunia to bloom exactly when you want it to requires intimate working knowledge of the plant's biology, local environmental conditions, and the relationship between them. The best results always come when you can combine hands-on experience with this vital knowledge."

The Structure of Gardening

In this book, Jim and I offer our different perspectives on gardening issues. I enjoy gardening for the sake of the beautiful plants, so my advice tends to focus on simple methods you can use to raise a great garden. Jim likes to know exactly how and why things work, so his answers explain the science behind the actions I recommend. In this way, Jim and I have tried to provide different kinds of information for gardeners with different interests. Although the flavour of our answers may differ, Jim and I share a common philosophy: get some basic knowledge before you begin, and learn from both your successes and your failures to enhance your future efforts.

The book is divided into six sections that follow a gardening season, in rough chronological and thematic order.

Soil
The foundation of all future efforts is soil. Without the right soil, in the garden or in containers, plants will fail to thrive right from the start. When our snapdragons started dying off, our colleague Clarence knew from experience what the problem was: "You're putting too much manure in the soil." Sure enough, once we cut down on the manure, our snapdragons roared back to life. It wasn't until years later, when the story came up again, that Jim pointed out why the manure was killing the snapdragons. "Clarence was right," Jim said, "snapdragons are sensitive to ammonia, and manure is full of it. Not only that, manure makes a great harbour for root-rot disease."

Choosing the Right Plants
If you've got good soil, almost anything will grow in it—but how do you choose what to plant?

While I always say that individual preference is the final arbiter, I do believe that some varieties are inherently superior to others. You should always do some research before you purchase plants, whether it's talking to friends, asking a grower you trust, or using a reliable book or catalogue.

Seeding

Once you've got your plants, you have to get them into the soil. But that's more complicated than simply poking seeds into the earth. While the most important step is to start with quality seeds, some require special treatment. I discovered, quite by accident, that tomato seeds need bottom heat when you start them indoors or they take forever to germinate. If I hadn't, just on a hunch, told Ted to wait a couple of days before throwing out the flats, I might never have discovered the difference in germination times.

Growing

For many gardeners, the growing process is the most enjoyable part of gardening. Watching tender seedlings reaching towards the sky, discovering the first flower buds, babying your beds with water, fertilizer, and careful hoeing...these are the things that make gardening magical. Naturally, it takes some work to cast those spells, and some knowledge to ease the way.

Troubleshooting

In the midst of raising your plants, it's almost inevitable that problems will arise. No season is perfect: if the bugs don't make an appearance, stray pets will surely use your flowerbeds as amusement parks, or the plant equivalent of the bubonic plague will ravage your hanging baskets. It's not easy to do, but try to take these setbacks with a sense of humour. They're part of the experience, after all, and there's a certain morbid fun in comparing garden horror stories.

Bedding-Plant Varieties

Finally, don't forget that much of the joy of gardening comes from experimenting with new plants and new varieties. Once your petunias and daisies are well established, give some of the huge, vibrant blooms of salpiglossis a try, or be daringly different with a cluster of cocoa-scented chocolate cosmos. There are literally thousands of choices, more than enough to make every garden a unique expression of its creator.

Opening Doors

Although every gardener experiences the occasional disaster, I believe that there's no such thing as a "black thumb." Whether you're trying to grow a single huge sunflower or lush, expansive beds of Bingo pansies, your best resource is solid growing information—and, of course, the ability to persevere. Relish your mistakes along with your successes! The questions each catastrophe raises inevitably lead down a garden path bordered with lush rows of colourful annuals. Or, as Jim might say, "each question is a doorway to truth." So open a few doors with some practical advice and the science behind it.

CHAPTER 1 &
SOIL

Without the right soil, in the garden or in

containers, plants will wither on the vine.

Sometimes the right soil is untouched clay loam;

sometimes it's not soil at all, but a soilless mix.

Tilling soil, adding organic matter, testing its pH

level, and even reaching down to squeeze it—all

of these actions give your plants the solid and

nurturing earth they need to thrive.

Soil

Why is good soil so important?

Lois ❖ Good soil is the foundation of a good garden. Grab a fistful of your soil and give it a good squeeze. Does it hold together or fall apart? If it holds together, is it still soft and springy or does it feel like a lump of clay? What colour is it?

If you have a nice, dark clump of earth that you can easily crumble between your fingers, you're well on your way. Otherwise, your first step should be to improve your soil quality.

Jim ❖ You simply can't grow a successful garden in bad soil. Creating and maintaining good soil may take some work, but no other gardening job is more important. Loam is the ultimate goal—loam is the blend of sand, silt, clay and organic matter.

What is good soil?

Lois ❖ Soil—both garden soil and potting soil—should serve your plants' needs. Good soil anchors the roots firmly, but is loose and porous enough to allow them to grow and branch. It retains moisture, but has adequate drainage. It's neither too acidic nor too alkaline, and contains all the nutrients your plants require.

How can I tell if I have good potting soil?

Lois ❖ Like good garden soil, potting soil should provide your plant with a healthy medium in which to grow—one that can hold moisture and nutrients while being loose enough for root growth.

To check potting-soil quality, fill a small pot with your soil and water it thoroughly. Within a minute or so, the water should begin to drain through the holes at the bottom, leaving the soil moist and springy. If you find yourself with a pot full of soupy muck, try a different brand next time!

Jim ❖ Like garden soil, good potting soil must have sufficient weight to anchor the plant without getting too compacted. It should have a nice, even texture and be free of weeds, insects, and disease. It pays to remember the brands that work well for you—and even more important to remember those that don't!

Garden Soil: Composition

What is in garden soil?

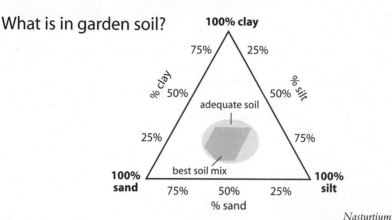

Potting Soil: Composition

What is potting soil composed of?

Lois ❖ The basic components in potting soil are peat moss, vermiculite, perlite, dolomitic lime, and a wetting agent.

Jim ❖ Here's a basic breakdown of the components in a high-quality potting soil (percentages will vary):

- blonde coarse peat moss: 50-60 % 0.5 m³
- perlite: 30-40 % 0.25 m³
- vermiculite (horticultural grade 2) 0.25 m³
- dolomitic lime (fine not coarse) 2–5 kg (depending on peat moss)
- wetting agent: 85 g

Regular Garden-Soil Mix

- 1 part field soil
- 1 part sphagnum peat moss
- 1 part perlite

Growers have replaced peat moss with such things as bark, coconut fibre, or even rice hulls with good success.

*Nasturtium
'Hermine Grashoff'*

What is peat moss?

Lois ❖ Peat moss is the organic material that provides the base for potting soil. It is partially decayed plant material from peat bogs.

Jim ❖ Peat moss forms in different layers in a bog. The upper layer, called blonde peat moss, is the best for use in potting soil. Light brown in colour and spongy to the touch, it is fibrous and has excellent moisture retention.

- Peat moss absorbs moisture and nutrients, keeping them in the soil where they can be used by plants.
- Peat moss loosens and aerates soils.
- Commercial potting mixtures contain 50 to 60% peat moss.
- Canada has more than 25% of the world's approximately 400 million hectares of peatland.
- Sphagnum peat bogs occupy 1% of the Earth's surface.
- The Canadian sphagnum peat-moss industry currently harvests on 16,000 hectares.
- Canadian peat, regarded as among the best-quality peat in the world, is sold to markets in the United States and Japan as well as across Canada.
- Sphagnum peat moss can hold 20 to 30 times its dry weight in water. (10 kg of peatmoss can weigh 300 kg when wet. Wow!) Cotton, by comparison, can hold only up to 6 times its own weight in water.

Source: Canadian Sphagnum Peat Moss Association

What is perlite?

Lois ❖ Perlite is a material that increases the porosity of soil, which, in turn, increases the drainage.

Jim ❖ Perlite is a volcanic rock mined mainly in Arizona. The hard, grey particles are heated in furnaces to temperatures of 1000°C, until they expand and pop like popcorn. Perlite is used in potting soil and in gardens as a lightweight alternative to sand. It does absorb some moisture, but it's used mostly to increase drainage, which in turn allows more air space into the mix.

What is vermiculite?

Lois ❖ Vermiculite is added to soil to help it retain nutrients and moisture.

Jim ❖ Vermiculite is a mica-type rock, shiny and flaky, with many plate-like sheets stacked tightly together. When heated to 1000°C, it expands like an accordion. Unlike perlite, which increases drainage in potting soils, vermiculite holds moisture and nutrients in its wafer-like structure. Be careful to use only horticultural-grade vermiculite in your garden, though, because construction-grade may contain toxic fire-retardant materials.

What is dolomitic lime?

Lois ❖ Dolomitic lime raises the pH level of soil. It neutralizes the acidity of the peat moss in potting soil.

Jim ❖ Dolomitic lime is a combination of magnesium carbonate ($MgCO_3$) and calcium carbonate ($CaCO_3$), both nutrients essential to plant growth. The term "lime" also refers to several other compounds:

- Lime—$CaCO_3$—calcium carbonate: This is almost as effective as dolomite when added to soil.

- Hydrated lime—$Ca(OH)_2$—calcium hydroxide: Some plants are sensitive to hydrated lime and may burn, but pH levels will increase. This is somewhat dangerous to handle—use with care.

- Quick lime—CaO—calcium oxide: This has a greater burn problem than hydrated lime, but will also increase the pH levels in your soil. Handle it with extreme caution.

- Gypsum—$Ca(SO_4)_2$—calcium sulphate: Gypsum has little effect on pH levels, but it does give clay soils more porosity.

What is a wetting agent?

Lois ❖ Wetting agents are chemicals added to potting mixtures to help them to absorb water.

Jim ❖ In effect, wetting agents make your water "wetter." They do this by breaking down the water surface tension. Instead of the water "beading" on the soil surface, the chemicals allow it to spread out into a film. This allows it to penetrate potting soil more evenly and thoroughly. Without wetting agents, you will have a hard time moistening the peat moss in the soil, and dry pockets will form in sections of the mix. All professional potting soils have wetting agents incorporated into the mixture.

Making Your Own Potting Soil

People sometimes ask me how to make their own potting soil. They usually have the mistaken impression that they can dig up some soil in their backyards, add a few extra ingredients, and end up with the kind of mix you'd buy at the store—only much cheaper. They're surprised when I tell them that "potting soil" is a bit of a misnomer, because most commercial potting soil doesn't contain any soil at all! Soilless potting mix first gained wide acceptance back in the '60s, thanks to some pioneering work at Cornell University. It took another 15 years or so, however, before the notion gained acceptance in the Hole household. When my husband Ted first suggested we start growing bedding plants and vegetable seedlings without soil, I thought he was crazy. Even after Ted showed me the research, I found it hard to stand by and watch it happen. As he made up the potting mix, I asked, "Don't you think we should throw a *little* soil in there?"

California Poppy 'Thai Silk Rose Chiffon'

Despite my reservations, the plants grew beautifully. The new mix had other clear advantages as well. It weighed much less than soil, which in turn made the seedling flats much easier to handle. It freed us from the annual chore of gathering soil and pasteurizing it, load by monotonous load.

On some cold winter afternoons, I feel a little nostalgic for the warm, musty smell of soil in the pasteurizer. Even if I miss the smell, though, I certainly don't miss all that extra work!

If you'd like to mix your own potting soil, you can buy the separate components and concoct your own unique blend. You might even include a bit of topsoil (in fact, recent research suggests that I might have been right on that count!). With so many excellent, affordable mixes on the market, though, it's simply not worth the bother—if you ask me!

I would really like to try making my own potting soil. What should I keep in mind?

Lois ❖ Make sure you're not doing it to save money, because you won't! It's often both difficult and costly to gather together all of the necessary ingredients. Even at the greenhouse we don't mix our own potting soil. We give precise specifications to our suppliers, and let them do the dirty work!

Jim ❖ If you're really keen on experimenting, there's no need to start right from scratch. Take a commercial mix and add things here and there. Maybe you're like Mom and would like to throw in a handful or two of garden soil. Or maybe you'd like to see how your seedlings would perform with a bit more peat moss in the mix. If you do decide to add compost or garden soil, however, be sure to pasteurize it first.

When you make your own mixture, you need to follow a few basic guidelines. The mixture should:

• not be too dense or easily compacted.

• contain plenty of perlite (30-40%), especially for plants prone to root rot (you can use sand, but the mixture may become too heavy).

• be pH balanced. Most potting soil should have a pH of 5.8–6.5.

• be disease and insect free. Peat moss, perlite, and vermiculite are all essentially clean.

Measure everything carefully, and keep detailed notes. If you don't know precisely what's in your mix, you won't be able to duplicate it next time.

What is pasteurization? Is it the same as sterilization?

Lois ❖ Think of pasteurization as a cleaning process. With pasteurization, you heat the soil enough to destroy most harmful microorganisms. You must pasteurize your garden soil if you plan to use it as a component of your potting mixture; otherwise you risk bringing weeds, pests, and soilborne diseases into your home.

Jim ❖ When you pasteurize your soil, the heat destroys harmful soil microorganisms while sparing many beneficial ones. Beneficial microorganisms break down different chemical components, making them available to your plants, and help to prevent disease organisms from getting re-established in the mix. Sterilization involves higher temperatures than pasteurization and destroys the good microorganisms along with the bad. High temperatures also precipitate toxic nitrates out in the mix.

How do I pasteurize my soil?

Lois ❖ The best way to pasteurize your soil is to "cook" it in your oven. A customer once told me that she would place her soil in an old roasting pan and leave it in a warm oven overnight. One night her husband woke her up, furious because his midnight snack had turned out to be a pan full of dirt!

Jim ❖ Bake your soil in a large, shallow pan at 82°C (180°F) for 30 minutes.

How do I avoid sterilizing when I'm trying to pasteurize?

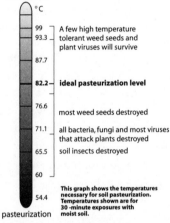

sterilization

°C

99	A few high temperature
93.3	tolerant weed seeds and plant viruses will survive
87.7	
82.2	**ideal pasteurization level**
76.6	most weed seeds destroyed
71.1	all bacteria, fungi and most viruses that attack plants destroyed
65.5	soil insects destroyed
60	
54.4	

pasteurization

This graph shows the temperatures necessary for soil pasteurization. Temperatures shown are for 30 -minute exposures with moist soil.

Lois ❖ Be sure not to overheat the soil. If you allow it to get warmer than 90°C, it is too hot; you'll be sterilizing rather than pasteurizing.

Jim ❖ This *Soil Pasteurization* graph should help.

I mixed my own potting soil last summer, but my plants grew poorly in it. What did I do wrong?

Lois ❖ There's a good chance that you either used inferior components, or mixed them in incorrect proportions. Think of your potting soil as a recipe: if you start off with poor ingredients, or you don't measure them carefully, you're just not going to be happy with the result. You have to give your plants the best possible start, especially with the mix they're growing in!

Jim ❖ Many different factors can cause a bad mixture!

• Poor sanitary practices when making your mixture. Make sure your work area is clean. If you add unpasteurized soil to your mixture, you'll almost certainly contaminate it with pests.

• Too dense a mix. Without sufficient porosity, the roots will not have enough air and space in which to grow. This usually means you're using too little perlite (or too fine a grade), or the wrong kind of peat moss. Sedge and hypnum peat moss, for example, aren't as fibrous as blonde peat moss. They are much more likely to get compacted.

• pH imbalance. If you don't add lime to your mix, then you'll fail to neutralize the acidity of the peat moss. At the same time, you don't want to add more lime than necessary. Your plants won't grow well if your mix is too acidic or too basic.

- Improper storage. If you store your potting mix near weed killer, for example, the weed killer can contaminate it.
- Excessive salt levels. This happens when you add too much fertilizer or unprocessed manure, which can "burn" your plants.

Why can't I get my potting soil to absorb water?

Lois ❖ If your potting soil is not absorbing water, then its components are unbalanced.

Jim ❖ Most potting-soil mixtures contain a lot of sphagnum peat moss, which is difficult to wet initially. Peat moss tends to repel water, which is why professional mixtures contain wetting agent.

Soil Tests

What is a soil test, and when should I get one?

Lois ❖ A soil test measures the various components that make up your soil and will determine if it is pH balanced. You should get your soil tested if you have a very large garden or acreage, or if you have a history of plants growing poorly in a specific area despite proper care.

Jim ❖ If you have specific problem areas in your garden, it's a good idea to do a soil test. You can learn as much from a soil test as you would from several years of trial and error.

Petunia 'Marco Polo Traveller'

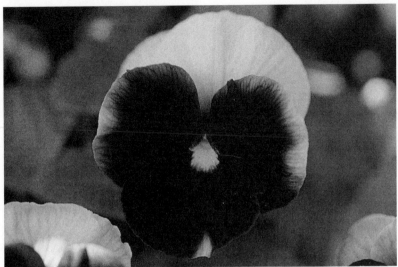

Pansy 'Imperial Beaconsfield'

What will a soil test tell me?

Jim ❖ A basic soil test tells you:

- levels of the major nutrients: nitrogen (N), phosphorus (P), and potassium (K) (these are the 3 numbers on a fertilizer label; thus, 10-52-10 is 10N-52P-10K).

- levels of the minor nutrients: iron (Fe), molybdenum (Mo), sulphur (S), magnesium (Mg), and calcium (Ca).

- the pH level: the level of acid or base of the soil.

- salt: plants can be burned if the levels are too high. (Some species, called halophytes, are much less sensitive than other plants; they tend to grow along salty marshes, and some even expel salt, leaving tiny amounts of salt on the leaves.)

- soil texture: this changes depending on the amount of sand, silt, clay, and organic matter.

For farmers, it could be very expensive *not* to test soil. For example, a deficiency of 20 kg of nitrogen per hectare adds up to a 10,000-kg shortage on a 500-hectare farm. That shortfall could result in catastrophic crop-yield losses.

Thankfully, the stakes aren't quite as high for home gardeners. However, if you're having trouble growing healthy plants, it's worth spending a few dollars to test and improve your soil.

Adding to the Soil

Does adding perlite to clay-like garden soil help it drain better? Is it the best solution for poor drainage?

Lois ❖ It's one solution, but it's not the best or cheapest alternative. You'd be better off adding sand, peat moss, manure, and compost.

Jim ❖ Perlite does help clay soil to drain better. However, perlite particles aren't very strong and can break down very quickly, especially if you work the soil with a rototiller. The other problem with perlite is that you need a tremendous amount to improve drainage, which is very expensive. It also blows away very easily in light winds. Instead, I recommend using coarse sand and plenty of organic matter. It's far cheaper and lasts much longer.

A product called gypsum (calcium sulphate) also helps drainage by causing the clay to form into columns.

Grower's edge

If you have trouble wetting your potting soil, try immersing the entire pot in a bucket of water. Leave it until it stops bubbling, then remove it and allow the excess water to drain. After that, your soil should absorb water much more easily, provided you never allow it to dry out completely.

Verbena 'Peaches and Cream'

I think that my soil is deficient in iron. What should I do?

Lois ❖ If you're really worried, you might consider investing in a soil test. However, if you believe your plants aren't absorbing enough iron, the problem might just be the pH of your soil. If your soil is too alkaline, the iron won't be available for your plants.

Jim ❖ Iron in alkaline soil is like sugar in an ice-cold glass of water—it doesn't dissolve easily. Lowering the soil's pH is like warming up that glass of water: the lower the pH, the more easily iron is absorbed. Before investing in a lab test for iron, you should check pH levels.

Can I just add rusty nails?

Lois ❖ No. It would take years before the iron in the nails began to break down and benefit your plants. Besides, who wants a garden full of rusty nails? You'd be risking tetanus every time you step into the garden! I have seen people pound old nails into their trees, though, which has some beneficial effect.

Jim ❖ The reason why nails won't help your plants but will help your trees has to do with where the nail is placed. Rusty nails release iron oxide, which is quite stable and therefore not readily available for absorption by the plant's roots. Roots absorb iron mostly in the form of ferric iron. Some of the iron oxide will eventually decompose into ferric iron, but this takes years. Pounding the rusty nail straight into the tree, however, puts the iron directly into the plant. But I don't recommend that you try this, because you risk introducing diseases and pests into the tree's tissues. Again, don't forget to check your soil pH.

Instead of adding rusty nails to your flowerbed, your best bet is to use chelated iron, which is readily available at most garden centres. The process of chelation protects the iron from being deactivated by alkaline soils.

Petunia 'Yellow Madness'

Petunia 'Marco Polo Odyssey'

What should I do about evergreen needles in my flower beds? Is there any way to neutralize the acidity from the needles?

Lois ❖ Lime will balance out the acidity of the needles. It would take an awful lot of evergreen needles, however, to significantly lower a soil's pH. Test your soil before assuming that acidity is the problem.

Jim ❖ Use dolomitic lime, because it contains both calcium and magnesium (two important plant nutrients). Be sure to buy a fine grade; otherwise the lime will react too slowly in the soil.

However, if you've got a flowerbed that's doing poorly underneath an evergreen tree, don't necessarily blame the needles! Often acidity is not the problem. Evergreens are shady, and their roots absorb a great deal of water. Even if the pH is perfectly balanced, you'll have a hard time growing anything under or near your tree.

Grower's edge

Sometimes the nose knows good soil. I'll never forget the first time Ted took me out to the site of our new farm, on the bank of St. Albert's Sturgeon river. He scooped up a handful of soil, smelled it, looked at me and said, "This is number-one soil." A rich, earthy smell is a great indicator of good soil.

My neighbour heard that adding sulphur to the garden would help her plants. What effect does sulphur have?

Lois ❖ Your neighbour is right—if the soil is too basic. Adding sulphur will make the soil more acidic, which is great for the many plants that prefer neutral soil.

Jim ❖ You can add sulphur for two different reasons: to lower the soil pH or to increase the amount of sulphur in sulphur-deficient soils. The sulphur you add must be very fine (microfine or superfine) in order to react quickly with your soil. It can take months for your soil to absorb coarse sulphur. Use iron sulphate, which reacts quickly with the soil.

Cosmos 'Sonata White'

Should I add lime to my soil?

Lois ❖ If you make your own potting soil with peat moss, add fine dolomitic lime a few weeks before using it, since lime takes a while to react in the soil. Be sure to use fine lime or else it will react too slowly to do any good. If you're adding the lime directly into your garden, do it in the fall after everything's cleaned up, or first thing in the spring. Lime doesn't solve all gardening problems, but it is good for neutralizing acid soils.

Jim ❖ Lime adjusts the pH of a soil by neutralizing the acidity of components like peat moss. Unless your soil is acidic, lime is often not required.

How much sulphur/lime to add to soil to change pH levels
GARDEN SULPHUR* 0.5 kg/100 m² (acidifier—to lower ph)

desired pH change	sands	loam	clay
8.5–6.5	46	57	68
8.0–6.5	27	34	46
7.5–6.5	11	18	23
7.0–6.5	2	3	6

* although sulphur is effective it is slow to react to soil

LIMESTONE 0.5 kg/100 m² (basifier—to increase pH)

desired pH change	sandy loam	loam	silt loam	clay
4.0–6.5	115	160	193	230
4.5–6.5	96	133	193	230
5.0–6.5	78	105	128	151
5.5–6.5	60	78	91	105
6.0–6.5	32	41	50	55

Sweet Pea 'Gwendoline'

My mom always throws her eggshells into the garden, because she says the calcium is good for the soil. Is she right?

Lois ❖ Most soil already contains plenty of calcium. However, adding eggshells to your garden or compost certainly beats sending them to the landfill.

I've been throwing eggshells into my soil for years. I once accidentally scored a direct hit on our German Shepherd, Sal, who was snoozing in my flowerbed!

Jim ❖ Eggshells won't have a big impact on the calcium in your soil. On the other hand, they certainly don't do any harm. So by all means, add them to your compost, but don't expect them to perform miracles in the garden.

Grower's *edge*

If you want to really test Mom's theory, you might try adding crushed eggshells when you transplant tomato seedlings. Tomatoes need a lot of calcium, so they would be the most likely plants to reap the benefits.

CHAPTER 2
CHOOSING ANNUALS

*You can't get a silk purse from a sow's ear…nor
can you grow a prize-winning geranium from an
inferior variety. Better breeding techniques have
developed plants with characteristics far in ad-
vance of their predecessors. More vibrant colours
in a wider palette, increased resistance to pests
and disease, drought and frost tolerance—all good
reasons to investigate a catalogue or two before
you purchase plants. That used to be one of my
favourite jobs, until I handed it over to my future
daughter-in-law, Valerie, who was still in high
school at the time. She took to it so handily that
she now does all of the bedding-plant ordering
for us. Whenever Jim and I have a bedding-
plant question we can't answer, she's an
excellent resource.*

What are the main factors I should consider when choosing varieties?

Lois ❖ I could spend the rest of the book answering this question! There are so many things to consider, but the most important points are how much room you have and how much sunlight your garden receives. Allow yourself plenty of time to shop around. It helps to arm yourself with a good reference book, so that you'll know which varieties will suit your needs. Past that, it's all a matter of personal taste!

Jim ❖ When choosing any plant, but especially annuals, look for stocky, well-branched specimens with dark-green leaves. Pop the plant out of its pot and check the roots. They should be white and out to the edge of the pot. Some plants (like marigolds and petunias) can bloom in the packs, but not all will (like gotedia or lavatera).

What is the difference between an annual and a perennial?

Lois ❖ An annual is a plant that goes from seed to bloom and back to seed in a single season. Perennials take much longer to complete their life cycle, often growing for several seasons before producing a single bloom. In short, you have to plant annuals every year—although several varieties (like pansies, cosmos, calendula, and annual poppies) self-sow so readily that they spring up again the following season without any help at all.

Jim ❖ That's a great definition, Mom. Of course, climate plays a key role in what we call an annual or a perennial. Many perennial plants from warmer climates are grown as annuals in Canada, like verbena, kniphofia, portulaca, and ice plant.

Why should I plant annuals year after year, when I could plant perennials instead?

Lois ❖ I hear variations of this question all the time! People have the idea that perennials are less expensive in the long run and require less work. However, if you compare the purchase prices, annual bedding plants represent wonderful value. And because they grow so quickly and dependably, annuals can actually be much easier to grow successfully.

I tell people that it's not a question of choosing one or the other. Plant some of each! There's a special pleasure in seeing your favourite perennials return each spring, but that's no reason to deny yourself the vibrant, long-lasting colour that annuals can bring to your garden.

Jim ❖ Annuals, unlike perennials, bloom from spring to fall. Perennials generally have a blooming period of only 2 to 3 weeks. Annuals also give you the opportunity to start over each spring. You can take last year's bed of marigolds and plant it in Wave petunias this year. They are less work and provide great curb appeal to your home.

Snapdragon 'La Bella Yellow'

Shopping for Bedding Plants

When is the best time to shop for bedding plants? When is it too late for it to be worthwhile?

Lois ❖ Last year, a fellow phoned on July 28 asking if it was too late for him to buy bedding plants. I told him to head straight for a garden centre! You won't find the same selection in July that you'd find in May, but the plants that are there will be much bigger and ready to go. At our greenhouse, we grow larger plants specifically for late-summer sales. These are great for what my daughter-in-law Valerie calls "instant colour."

Jim ❖ When buying plants in the summer, be sure to choose only large, fully branched plants. That way, you won't have to wait long for results. You can also buy pre-planted patio containers, which instantly add lush mounds of vibrant colour to your yard.

Buying in the summer has its advantages. For instance, garden mums are only available in late July or early August. By shopping for plants then, you can give your garden a whole new look for the latter part of the season.

Where should I shop? What features should I look for in a greenhouse?

Lois ❖ You can often predict the quality of the plants the moment you walk through the door. If the building itself seems clean and organized and has knowledgable staff, you can be sure that the plants receive the care they need.

Jim ❖ Healthy, vibrant-looking plants are the first thing you should look for, but the staff is also key. There must be enough of them, and they need to know the business. If you have a question, or are looking for suggestions, there should be someone who's ready and able to help you. You should also ask if they grow the plants themselves or if they are brought in.

Marigold 'Bonanza Harmony'

How many plants do I need to fill a specific area? Is there an overall formula?

Lois ❖ It all depends on the variety. The tag or seed packet should give you a good idea of how big the plants will grow. I always tell people to plant thickly, leaving just enough room for each plant to grow to its fullest. Nothing beats a nice, solid flowerbed for lots of lush colour.

Jim ❖ Mom's right—there's no magic formula. You need to know how big the plants will be when they mature. For many of the popular annuals, though, you can expect to plant 30–35/m² (3–4/sq. ft.).

What is a flat? A pack? What is the difference in pack sizes?

Lois ❖ A flat is just the tray in which you carry around packs of young plants. It looks like a baking pan. Packs, on the other hand, resemble smaller muffin tins, with their individual cells.

Jim ❖ A flat is the rectangular container (plastic tray) that holds the packs. Most seedlings are sold in packs—thin, rectangular plastic containers holding from 1 to 6 (or more) individual plants.

Packs come in many different sizes, each with its own number. For example, the Jumbo 606 has six large packs per flat, with six cells per pack. In other words, a flat with a 606 insert holds a total of 36 seedlings. We use the Jumbo 606 because it allows us to grow a much larger and healthier plant. The most common size you see at a greenhouse is usually the 1206, which has half the space per plant but holds 72 plants. A 1501 has 15 individual packs with only one cell each. This would be used for larger, more mature plants.

Why are some annuals sold in packs of six, while others are available only in single containers?

Lois ❖ Some plants just wouldn't survive if you tried to crowd them into a six-pack. Fast-spreading plants like the Wave petunias or large growers like Fiesta impatiens would become spindly and root-bound in no time at all. These plants need room to grow!

Jim ❖ People are so used to buying six plants at a time, they often won't even look at single plants. As a result, greenhouses face a real balancing act when deciding on pack sizes. In the end, we have to do what's best for the plants and have faith that our customers will trust our judgement. In other words, if a certain plant is only available in single containers, there's probably a good reason.

Should I buy small plants or more mature ones?

Lois ❖ It depends on your budget and on the time of year. If you're starting your garden nice and early, and don't mind waiting a few weeks for flowers, small plants can give you more for your money. If you're eager for quick results, though, buy the largest, most mature plants you can afford, so long as they haven't outgrown their containers.

Jim ❖ I tell people to set aside at least part of their garden, and part of their budget, for larger plants. If you buy larger plants you don't need as many, and you can plant them further apart and still get "instant" colour. If you break it down to cents per season, large plants are often cheaper.

When I'm looking at a whole table full of seedlings, how do I decide which to buy?

Lois ❖ If they're all healthy and thriving, and they should be, it won't make much difference which one you buy. Always be sure, though, that the plants are full and evenly branched.

Jim ❖ Pick up a pack and examine the plants from all sides. If they look strong, symmetrical, and pest free, put the pack in your shopping cart! Well-established, attractive seedlings will grow into well-established, attractive mature plants, assuming you care for them adequately.

While shopping, how do I recognize which plants are healthy?

Lois ❖ If you buy a plant that's spindly, wilted, or damaged in any way, it will almost certainly disappoint you in the long run.

Jim ❖ Usually, you can tell at a glance whether or not a plant is healthy. Avoid plants with discoloured or wilted leaves, spindly stems, or, in extreme cases, broken branches or insect damage.

How do I design a flowerbed? Should I mix colours, heights and varieties, or use mass plantings?

Lois ❖ I always tell people to keep it simple. To my eye, nothing matches the appeal of a mass planting. Find a variety that doesn't require too much maintenance, choose your favourite colour, and then fill the bed with it. You'll be rewarded with a spectacular display of vibrant colour and lush, even greenery. I have a flowerbed in front of my house that I fill with masses of Atlantis marigolds—it's stunning!

Jim ❖ Mom's right. Why not keep things simple? Life is complicated enough as it is.

But keeping it simple doesn't mean keeping it boring! Don't stick with the same old varieties year after year. There are always plenty of new hybrids and colours to choose from. For instance, last year I convinced one customer to try Wave petunias for the first time, and she couldn't believe the results.

Approach your garden the way a child approaches a colouring book— be bold, have fun, and don't be afraid to colour outside the lines once in a while!

I've wondered about trying some less common annuals, such as godetia, but they never look very appealing. Are they worth considering?

Lois ❖ Absolutely! If you stick with only those plants that look nice in the greenhouse, you don't know what you're missing. Some of the most gorgeous annuals look positively drab as young plants. Satin series godetia is a perfect example. If you put young godetia and marigold plants side by side in the greenhouse, people will flock to all of the beautiful blossoms on the marigolds. My mother always grew godetia, however, so I know how wonderful they are over the course of a season.

Jim ❖ New breeding work has greatly improved growth habit and flower quality and has also increased the number of blooms. Be sure to check out other less-common plants like Royale salpiglossis, Daybreak gazanias, candytuft, or lavatera. These and many other lesser-known bedding plants deserve a chance to put on a show in your garden.

some early-blooming plants

baby's breath
bachelor's button
carnation
cosmos
dianthus
flowering cabbage
   and kale
pansy
poppy
sweet pea
viola
wee willie

some later-blooming plants

asters
bells of Ireland
tall snapdragons
stocks
strawflowers
statice
scabiosa
sunflowers

I want to be able to cut fresh flowers from my garden all summer long. What varieties should I plant?

Lois ❖ There's no substitute for careful planning and accurate information. Some plants flower early in the season, others later. Some flowers bloom for shorter periods, while others continue to produce blossoms for months. If you want a good supply of flowers all season long, you'll have to find the right blend of varieties. The Bingo pansies are some of my favourite early cutflowers, and I have a huge soft spot for asters.

Jim ❖ When we prune our Madness or Wave petunias, we often put the stems in water—they make an excellent, if less well-known, cutflower. Find out which varieties bloom early and which bloom late, make sure you have a balance between the two, and don't be afraid to try different things.

I love butterflies. How do I attract them to my garden?

Lois ❖ Just plant plenty of their favourite flowers. Among the annuals they like best are asters, nicotianas, petunias and thunbergia. Wave and Tidal Wave petunias work well and provide some beautiful colour to your beds.

Jim ❖ Butterflies have an astonishing sense of sight and smell, and can detect their favourite flowers from far off. They will begin to appear almost as soon as your plants are in bloom. As long as your garden provides a plentiful source of nectar, you can be sure that the butterflies will drop by for regular visits.

Grower's edge

One day, an elderly gentleman walked into our greenhouse carrying a sturdy pair of scissors. It seems he needed one more impatiens to fill out his planter, and by gosh, one was all he was going to buy!

Annual fall mums

Which annual varieties make the best dried flowers?

Lois ❖ A lot of flowers remain colourful and attractive, and even fragrant, after they've been dried. Among my favourite dried flowers are sunflowers, carnations, salvia, Queen Anne's lace, xeranthemum, and stocks.

Jim ❖ You don't need any special equipment or expertise to try your hand at drying flowers. All you have to do is tie the stems together in small bunches, hang them upside-down in a dark, well-ventilated room, and wait for a few days.

Which annuals are the most fragrant?

Lois ❖ Fortunately, many of my favourite flowers also smell wonderful. Try planting stocks, sweet peas (especially the Gwendoline variety), yellow or white pansies, dark-purple petunias, white alyssum, heliotrope, white nicotiana, and certain carnations. I guarantee that the fragrance will give you extra incentive to spend time in your garden.

Jim ❖ Fragrance can be like colour—you don't want your plants clashing or competing with each other, or overpowering your senses. When planting particularly fragrant annuals, be sure to give each variety enough breathing room.

some varieties for drying

bells of Ireland
  (for striking accents)
carnation
celosia
gomphrena
helipterum
larkspur
nigella (both the flowers
  and the seed pods)
Queen Anne's lace
Salvia (*S. farinacea* and
  S. horminum)
scabiosa (the seed pods of
  S. stellata—paper moon)
statice
stock
strawflower
sunflower
xeranthemum

some varieties for fragrance

alyssum
  (especially white flowers)
carnation
  (certain varietes only)
evening scented stock
heliotrope
nicotiana
pansy
  (usually the yellow and
  white blooms are scented)
petunia
  (dark purple
  flowers mostly)
stock
sweet pea

How can I encourage hummingbirds to visit my garden?

Lois ❖ I've never met anyone who doesn't love hummingbirds! If you give them easy access to the flowers they like, chances are you'll be able to glimpse them from time to time. Hanging baskets make the flowers more visible to passing hummingbirds, and at the same time give you a better view of any birds you might attract.

Jim ❖ Hovering requires a lot more energy than flying, so hummingbirds need to eat about four times every hour. If you offer them a reliable source of food, they can be extremely faithful customers.

If you think like a hummingbird, you can recognize their favourite flowers. The blossoms project out into the air, so that the birds can sip from them without catching their wings on the foliage. Often they're trumpet-shaped, to accommodate a hummingbird's bill. Among hummingbirds' favourite annuals are impatiens, nicotiana, petunia, and fuchsia. One or two well-placed feeders will also help make your garden a popular stop for these very small, very hungry birds.

Pansy 'Purple Rain'

Summer Madness Petunia

What plants should I choose for my hanging baskets or moss planters?

Lois ❖ For moss planters, you'll want a few upright, mounding plants like Designer geraniums or Bonanza marigolds to fill out the top, and plenty of colourful trailing flowers like Sapphire lobelia, trailing Quartz verbena, or Sundial portulaca.

Hanging baskets look their best when they're filled with mounding or trailing annuals like fuchsias, Showstopper impatiens, or Wave petunias.

Of course, there are dozens of possible combinations. Let your imagination run wild!

Jim ❖ Remember to take into account how much sunshine your planter will receive. I recommend impatiens, lobelia, and fuchsia for planters in shadier, sheltered areas. Petunias, pansies, and marigold can handle more sunlight; however, keep in mind that the more sun your basket gets, the more water it will need.

Nolana 'Sky Blue'

How many plants do I need to make a hanging basket look full and lush?

Lois ❖ It all depends on the size of the basket and the kind of plant you want to use. We plant 5 to 7 plants in a 35-cm basket.

Grower's edge

While some parts of annuals like pansy petals and sunflower seeds are delicious, many plants are edible but not palatable. A few plants such as brugmansia, datura and castor bean (*Ricinus*) are highly toxic. Always check with your local poison centre if you aren't sure.

Are any bedding plants poisonous?

Lois ❖ Several bedding plants are poisonous, but I've never worried about toxicity when choosing annuals. It's extremely unlikely that a passing animal or child would eat enough plant material to suffer injury.

Jim ❖ Keep in mind that everything is poisonous if you eat enough of it. However, none of the common bedding plants are particularly toxic. Just the same, though, teach your young children that bedding plants are for seeing and smelling, not for tasting!

CHAPTER 3 🐾
SEEDING

Each seed is a tiny reservoir of potential, just
waiting to be unlocked. To realize that potential,
you've got to know what each seed needs: some
require a cold treatment, some like it hot. Others
need to be scuffed up a little, and an accommo-
dating few will surge to life with practically
no help at all. Don't balk at spending an extra
10 or 15 cents per seed when you know the
more expensive variety will top the other in both
quality and quantity of vibrant blooms.
With quality seed and the right knowledge,
germination rates—and the aesthetics of your
garden—will soar.

Is it better to grow my annuals from seeds, or should I just buy bedding plants?

Lois ❖ Let your interests be your guide! Growing annuals from seed is a great pastime, especially if you're eager to start gardening while there's still snow on the ground. However, some varieties are easier to start from seed than others. We had a heck of a time growing bells of Ireland from seed until we discovered, quite by accident, that they require a cold treatment before they will germinate. If they hadn't been set down on a cold concrete floor, we never would have discovered what were doing wrong!

Jim ❖ Mom's right. There's nothing more frustrating than planting a tray full of seeds only to be faced with a barren pack even after weeks of care. To avoid disappointment, choose easy-to-germinate seed like marigolds and nasturtiums, and buy bedding plants if you want to grow the more demanding annuals like begonias and alyssum. Of course, if you like the challenge of growing the picky species from seed, by all means, give them a try. Just take the time to learn a little about their needs.

Pansy 'Baby Bingo Midnight'

Seeding Dates for Flowers in Cooler Zones

Early February To Mid-February
Begonias (tuberous)
Browallia
Geraniums
Larkspur
Pansy
Petunias (double-flowering)
Viola

Mid-February To End Of February
Begonias (fibrous)
Dianthus
Dusty Miller
Marigold (medium-height varieties)
Petunias (single-flowering)
Phlox
Salpiglossis
Salvia
Snapdragons

Early March To Mid-March
Ageratum
Alyssum
Balsam
Candytuft
Celosia

Chrysanthemum (annual)
Cleome
Coleus
Dahlia
Dimorphotheca
Impatiens
Kennelworth Ivy
Marigolds (short varieties)
Matthiola
Mimulus
Nicotiana
Nierembergia
Nigella
Portulaca
Sanvitalia
Scabiosa
Statice
Torenia
Verbena
Xeranthemum

Mid-March To End Of March
Amaranthus
Asters
Calendula
Carnation (annual)
Dahlberg daisy
Flowering cabbage

Flowering Kale
Gazania
Godetia
Kochia
Lavatera
Lobelia
Marigolds (tall varieties)
Nemesia
Schizanthus
Stocks
Thunbergia

Early April To Mid-April
Canary Bird Vine
Centaurea
Clarkia
Cobaea
Cosmos
Gypsophila
Helianthus
Iceplant
Morning Glory
Nemophila
Poppy
Zinnia

Mid-April To Late April
Nasturtiums
Sweet Peas

When should I start my seeds?

Lois ❖ It depends on when you're going to transplant your seedlings outdoors. For example, here in St. Albert the average last spring-frost date is May 6. We transplant our pansies outside 3 weeks before that in mid-April 15. Pansy seedlings take about 14 weeks to grow from seed, so we start the seeds in mid-February. It takes a bit of planning, but it's worth it. By May last year, I had pots filled with Lavender Blue Baby Bingo pansies on my deck, and they recieved rave reviews.

Jim ❖ People spend a lot of time worrying about frost. They don't realize that many annuals need to be outside and growing in the early part of the growing season. More plants are finished off by heat and drought in the summer than by frost in May! In our experience is actually better to put annuals like pansies outside and cover them than to leave them indoors and have them stretch out from being too hot.

There's really no substitute for planning. Read your seed packets carefully, check on the average last spring-frost date for your area, and do the math for yourself.

What are the easiest annuals to start from seed?

Lois ❖ By and large, the bigger the seed is, the easier it is to grow. If you start off with larger seeds such as sweet peas, nasturtiums, and marigolds, you're almost guaranteed success. Once you've gotten the hang of it, you can move on to smaller seeds, which tend to be more challenging to grow.

Jim ❖ The sweet pea is the easiest annual to grow from seed. Not only is a sweet pea seed big, it's nearly indestructible! It doesn't mind if you give it too much water or too little. It's disease resistant and easy to handle because it's so big. On the other hand, tuberous and fibrous begonias are among the trickiest annuals to seed. The seeds are almost as small as dust particles. You can barely see them, let alone pick them up with your fingers. These seeds require consistently warm soil, and just the right amount of fertilizer; otherwise they starve. Raising begonias from seed is definitely a challenge compared to the easygoing sweet pea!

some annuals for direct seeding

African daisy
baby's breath
bachelor's button
calendula
canary bird vine
cosmos
four o'clock
kochia
lavatera
nasturtiums
poppies
sweet peas
sunflowers
viscaria
zinna

What are hybrid seeds?

Lois ❖ There are many different kinds of hybrid seeds. One hybrid seed tends to be very similar to the next, unlike non-hybrid seeds, which sometimes surprise you when they bloom! Hybrid seeds are more expensive than their non-hybrid cousins, but the extra pennies are worth it! Plants that grow from hybrid seeds tend to have all kinds of bonuses, like bigger and more colourful blooms, greater disease resistance, and better growth habit.

Jim ❖ Development of hybrid plants is a complex prodedure that ultimately, if everything goes right, results in very uniform varieties.

Birth of a Hybrid

Let's say, for instance, that you are a plant breeder, and you want to combine the intense red flower colour of one variety with the disease resistance of another.

First, you must select and isolate two parent lines: one with the intense colour and the other with the disease resistance. Each parent is inbred for several generations until the desirable traits (intense red and disease resistance) are expressed consistantly in each parent's offspring. At the end of these several generations, you then save seeds each parent line.

All of the flowers in one parent line will be uniformly intense red, while those in the other are uniformly disease resistant. At this point, you cross-pollinate the two parent lines. If you're *lucky* you'll create an intensely red-flowered, disease-resistant hybrid. Once this happens, you can continue to cross-pollinate your two pure parent lines year after year and produce consistent, high-quality hybrid seed every time.

Unfortunately, because of the painstaking, unpredictable nature of the process, hybrid seed tends to be more expensive than non-hybrid seed. However, measured against the results they produce, hybrid seeds often represent your best value.

Can I plant the seeds collected from hybrid plants?

Lois ❖ You can, but only if you're prepared for unpredictable (and often downright unsuccessful) results. Hybrid plants don't make good parents!

Jim ❖ Seeds taken from hybrid plants don't grow "true to type." In other words, if you save hybrid seed and grow it the following year, some of the resulting plants will look like each of the parents rather than the hybrid.

What is pelleted seed?

Lois ❖ Pelleting makes tiny or irregularly shaped seeds easier to handle. Each individual seed is coated with clay or a clay-like material, turning it into a uniform pellet.

Jim ❖ Commonly pelleted varieties include begonia, petunia, lisianthus, and dusty miller. Pelleting can delay germination a bit, because of the time it takes for water to penetrate the coating. However, it makes the seeding process much easier. With smaller seeds like alyssum and lobelia, you often plant 6 or more seeds in the same pot. The pelleted seed we use for these plants has 3 seeds clumped together in one pellet, making it much easier to sow.

What do I need to grow my own annuals from seed?

Lois ❖ First you need the very best-quality seeds. My mother-in-law, Grandma Hole, always said, "Only the rich can afford to buy cheap things!" If you start off with inferior seed, you might as well not even bother. Also, you'll want to give those seeds a good home, so be sure to buy a professional seedling mixture.

Jim ❖ You can start with as little as seeds, potting soil, flats, and a sunny window. If you're ready to get a bit more serious, though, it's worth investing in the right equipment

basic equipment checklist
• the best available seed
• the best-quality soilless mix (professional grade)
• a mister bottle
• clean plastic flats
• grow lights
• covers (plastic or fabric)
• fine-textured vermiculite to cover your seedlings
• a thermometer with a probe (an oven meat-thermometer works well)
• heating cables
• fungicides (optional)
• tags to label the different varieties

Pansy 'Baby Bingo Sky Blue'

What other factors are important for good germination?

Lois ❖ Even though I always emphasize the importance of watering, oxygen is just as important for your seeds. If you keep your flats saturated with water, your seeds will drown. You also need to check your seed packets to see if your seeds require special conditions to germinate.

Jim ❖ Oxygen and moisture must penetrate a seed's coat in order for it to germinate. Apart from that, different seeds have their own requirements. For example, the smallest seeds (like alyssum, begonia, coleus, and petunia) generally require light in order to germinate. Other seeds, such as larkspur, phlox, and verbena, prefer to germinate in the dark.

Some seeds actually need a little abuse to get started! In one process, scarification, the seed coats are cut or abraded in order to allow water and oxygen to penetrate. In another process, stratification, the seeds are stored in a cold, moist environment for several weeks or months, to simulate the passing of winter.

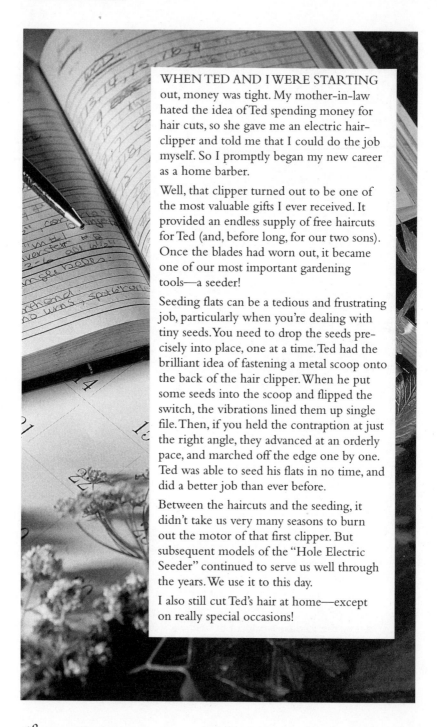

WHEN TED AND I WERE STARTING out, money was tight. My mother-in-law hated the idea of Ted spending money for hair cuts, so she gave me an electric hair-clipper and told me that I could do the job myself. So I promptly began my new career as a home barber.

Well, that clipper turned out to be one of the most valuable gifts I ever received. It provided an endless supply of free haircuts for Ted (and, before long, for our two sons). Once the blades had worn out, it became one of our most important gardening tools—a seeder!

Seeding flats can be a tedious and frustrating job, particularly when you're dealing with tiny seeds. You need to drop the seeds precisely into place, one at a time. Ted had the brilliant idea of fastening a metal scoop onto the back of the hair clipper. When he put some seeds into the scoop and flipped the switch, the vibrations lined them up single file. Then, if you held the contraption at just the right angle, they advanced at an orderly pace, and marched off the edge one by one. Ted was able to seed his flats in no time, and did a better job than ever before.

Between the haircuts and the seeding, it didn't take us very many seasons to burn out the motor of that first clipper. But subsequent models of the "Hole Electric Seeder" continued to serve us well through the years. We use it to this day.

I also still cut Ted's hair at home—except on really special occasions!

Do I need a special kind of soil for my seedlings?

Lois ❖ Yes! Even though you can get reasonably good results from regular potting soil, you'll have better luck if you use a special mix for your seedlings. I always use Ball Seedling Mix. It has just the right components for healthy seedlings.

Jim ❖ I agree wholeheartedly. For the best seedlings, you should always start off with the best soil.

Spend the few extra dollars and invest in a professional seedling soil. Regular potting soil is too coarse and variable to risk using on your seedlings.

What things can contaminate my seedlings?

Lois ❖ Take the time to practice good sanitation. You must be careful to work in a clean space with clean tools. And wash your hands, too!

Jim ❖ Disease can enter the picture at several points.

- Containers or other tools. Rinse your tools, plus any previously used flats or trays, in a 10%-bleach solution.

- Improper sanitation. Listen to Mom! Always wash your hands before working with your seedlings. Tobacco carries the mosaic virus, while certain foods like lettuce carry damping-off diseases.

- Unpasteurized soil. If you insist on adding garden soil or compost, pasteurize it first (see Chapter 1).

- The seeds themselves. Some diseases live in the seed or on the seed coat itself. Buy only the best-quality seeds.

- Dirty water or dirty watering cans (tap water is fine, provided it's not high in salts—sodium in particular).

Do I need to use pesticides to grow seedlings?

Lois ❖ No. Pesticides are not the answer. Ted and I used to grow our seedlings without using pesticides, and to this day, we still do. The key is sanitation, sanitation, sanitation! If you keep everything perfectly clean, you won't have to rely on chemicals.

Jim ❖ I agree. You don't need pesticides to grow your seedlings, especially if you use a professional seedling mixture. This is the key—garden soil introduces many unwanted potential problems for seedlings. Fungicides, on the other hand, can be an important investment. Even with the best sanitation, fungal diseases can occasionally find their way to your seedlings.

What is an inoculant? When should I use it?

Lois ❖ Inoculant is a black powder containing bacteria and is typically used to treat seeds of plants in the legume family. Along with peas and beans, the legumes include many bedding plants, such as sweet peas and lupines.

The bacteria provide the legumes nutrients to grow and produce more flowers and seeds. You'll want to use it to make the most of your legume plants! Most well-stocked garden centres carry inoculant.

Jim ❖ Although some fungi and bacteria attack plants, most are harmless. Still others are beneficial, including inoculants. One of the more common inoculants contains a genus of bacteria called *Rhizobia*, which forms a symbiotic relationship with legumes. The rhizobia infects the roots of legumes, and helps the plants utilize nitrogen from the soil. We've had good success using it on both garden peas, broad beans and sweet peas.

Plants cannot use nitrogen directly from the air. However, rhizobia can take atmospheric nitrogen and "fix" it into compounds that the plant can use. In turn, the plant provides nutrients necessary for the bacteria to live. It's a nice trade-off! Inoculant can be an excellent investment for your legumes. For the small amount you pay for the inoculant, you end up with a lot of valuable nitrogen in the soil.

I've heard Lois say to always plant thickly. Does this apply to seedlings as well?

Lois ❖ Sometimes I have to eat my own words! Many novice gardeners make the mistake of sowing seeds too closely in the pack. You may think you're saving money by buying less soil and fewer containers, but over-crowded seedlings tend to stretch and become weak and disease prone. They also just don't transplant well at all. In the end you'll not only waste your money, but your time as well.

It's best to space your seedlings out carefully and evenly in a flat. I like to use my trusty electric razor. You can also buy inexpensive hand-operated seeding gadgets at most garden centres.

Can I buy seed for all the bedding plants sold in the greenhouse?

Lois ❖ You can for many of them, but not all. Some varieties are only available as seed in the garden centre, and some are only available as bedding plants.

Jim ❖ When a new variety is first produced, information is initially provided to growers. Demand is high and seed production is limited, so generally all the seed that can be produced is sold to them. As production gradually increases and more seed is available, it is also sold to companies who package seed for retail sales, at which time it becomes available to you.

Of course, not all plants are grown from seed. Rather, they are vegetatively propagated, which means that they're grown directly from cuttings taken from stock plants.

Why are some seed varieties more costly than others? For example, why do new varieties generally cost more than older varieties?

Lois ❖ Well, you get what you pay for. High-quality seed that has been extensively tested will cost more than poorer-quality seed.

Jim ❖ Quality control is one factor, but there are others as well. It takes a great deal of time and labour to create a successful new hybrid. Pelleted seeds also cost a bit extra, but can save you a lot of time and effort.

Do seeds carry diseases?

Lois ❖ It's definitely possible. That's why I always tell gardeners to buy the highest-quality seed available. This doesn't eliminate disease, but it will reduce the incidence.

Jim ❖ Yes. Seeds can carry fungi, bacteria, and viruses. Fungi and bacteria can reside on the outside of the seed (on its coat) or within the seed, while viruses typically occur only within the seed. Seed-borne viruses become part of the genetic makeup of the seed and cannot be detected prior to seeding. Last year we had downy mildew on some of our alyssum—but fortunately, the alyssum grew out of the problem.

Fungi and bacteria are easier to detect, however, and seed companies use various methods to fix the problem. With lavatera, for example, some companies scrape off the outer seed coat in order to remove most of the fungus. Other seeds are treated in hot water, at temperatures just high enough to kill off any bacteria or fungi without harming the seeds themselves.

Pansy 'Bingo Red and Yellow'

CHAPTER 4 🌿
GROWING

While a simple regimen of watering, fertilizing, and weeding will keep most plants growing nicely, it doesn't hurt to take things to a more advanced level. Thanks to his university experiences, Jim made things a bit easier in the greenhouse by introducing us to growth regulators, chemicals that slowed down the plants that grew just a little too quickly to keep up with. Jim also discovered that the Mag-Amp slow-release fertilizer we were using at the time was way too high in phosphorus. While we couldn't afford to switch the more expensive (but more correctly balanced) liquid fertilizers at the time, we still had the knowledge, and when the business expanded sufficiently to make the switch feasible, we did it immediately.

Grow Lights

What are grow lights?
Do I need them and why?

Lois ❖ Grow lights are light bulbs that have been specifically designed to help plants to grow better. In some situations, grow lights can provide plants with their only source of light.

Unless you're gardening on a very large scale, you might find that the sun is the only grow light you need! In fact, when I first started in the greenhouse business, I never used grow lights. I just placed my seedling flats near a big, south-facing window. Over the years, I had good success—most of the time! Of course, any time you rely entirely on Mother Nature you can expect a few surprises!

If you're starting a lot of seedlings, or don't have adequate indoor light, grow lights can be a good investment.

Jim ❖ Actually, any light bulb is a grow light, since all light sources provide energy for plant growth. However, not all lights are created equal!

Standard incandescent bulbs (the type typically used in lamps around your home) emit too much infrared light (heat) to help plants thrive. Your seedlings end up overheating, and don't get enough of the cool blue light they need to grow well. Fluorescent lights provide more blue light. Because they are low in infrared light, you can place them close to your seedlings. They don't produce quite as wide a light spectrum as true grow lights, but they do the job just fine.

In our greenhouses we use HID (High Intensity Discharge) lights. Next to the sun itself, these are the ultimate grow lights—in fact, you can use them to grow tomatoes without any other source of light. However, HID lights can cost hundreds of dollars for a single fixture—a bit rich for the typical gardener!

A bright sunny window remains your least expensive option.
If you're just starting a flat or two of seedlings, it will provide all the light you need.

Grow Light Pros and Cons

REGULAR INCANDESCENT
Pros
Low initial cost, readily available

Cons
Inefficient and more costly to run
Heat may damage plants
Narrow light spectrum (because plants get far too much red light)

REGULAR FLUORESCENT
Pros
Moderate initial cost, ready availability
Cool (may be placed close to plants)
Much more efficient than incandescent
Provide more "blue" light

Cons
Do not provide adequate red light (which plants also need)
Higher initial cost for fixtures and bulbs
Produce far too little light energy for larger plants

CONSUMER GROW LIGHT
Pros
Provides a balanced spectrum of "blue" and "red" light, while consuming nearly the same amount of electricity as traditional fluorescent lights.

Cons
More expensive than regular fluorescent lights

HID LIGHTS
Pros
Provide full spectrum of light needed for plant growth

Cons
Very high initial cost may provide too much energy for young seedlings
The overall colour band is yellow or silver gray, making the plants appear less attractive to the human eye

SUNLIGHT
Pros
It's free!
Cons
We can't control where and when (or even if!) it will shine

Marigold 'Sweet Cream'

Temperature

What is the optimum soil temperature for germination?

Lois ❖ Every seed has an ideal temperature for germination, from 15-26°C. I try to keep my soil within this range, but it takes a lot of trial and error to get it right!

Jim ❖ For the most part, bedding plants fall into two categories: those which need cool soil for germination (15-20°C), and those which need warmer soil (21-26°C). For the best results, you should keep this temperature constant, day and night. The simplest way to do this is with heating cables. They're not that expensive and can be purchased at any good garden centre.

Remember that soil temperature can differ significantly from the air temperature. Monitor your flats with a temperature probe—it's well worth the few dollars it costs! Check your flats twice a day, in the morning and evening, by placing the probe at the depth of the seed—no deeper. This will tell you the exact soil temperature. At the greenhouse we use an infrared gun—just point and shoot for an instant soil-temperature reading—but that's well beyond most people's budget.

Is my windowsill too cold in the winter?

Lois ❖ Usually, the temperature on a windowsill fluctuates too much. Seeds prefer consistent warmth for germination.

Jim ❖ Cold air spills down the glass, chilling the soil overnight. Heating cables can reduce this problem.

Maintenance

How should I water my seedlings?

Lois ❖ Carefully! In the greenhouse, I put it this way: whoever waters the plants controls the profits. Gardeners make two main mistakes when watering seedlings: making the flats too wet (or not wet enough), and washing the seeds away to the edges of the flat by using too strong a stream of water.

Use a seedling nozzle on the end of your watering can, never a regular nozzle. Seedling nozzles produce a very fine droplet size that won't wash away the seeds. Even better, use a simple mister bottle, which produces the finest droplets and reduces the risk of washing away the seeds.

Jim ❖ I agree with Mom—you do have to water seedlings carefully. The job is easier if you thoroughly moisten your seeding mixture before adding the seeds. After that, you only need to replace any moisture that's lost. Don't give the flats any more water than that. Seeds can literally drown if they're constantly waterlogged. They need both moisture *and* oxygen to germinate.

Once you've moistened the soil in the flat with a watering can, you only need to add enough water to keep it from drying out. Keep your mister bottle handy, and spray the surface from time to time.

Give your seedlings the moisture they need!

• Moisten the soil mix thoroughly before planting.

• Sow the seeds.

• Spray the soil surface well with a mister bottle.

• Cover the flats with clear or black plastic or fabric until the seedlings emerge.

• Mist every time the soil surface begins to show signs of drying out.

Water wand

My seedlings tend to become leggy. Some of them even flop over. What causes this?

Lois ❖ Leggy seedlings are usually caused by a shortage of light, combined with warm day temperatures and cool night temperatures. Be careful to maintain a constant temperature as your seeds germinate. Once the seedlings emerge, however, reduce the soil and air temperature as soon as possible.

If you don't check your flats regularly, it's easy to miss this critical transition. I've checked flats at nine in the morning and returned at three in the afternoon to find the seedlings fully emerged. They're just like teens—you blink and they're two feet taller!

Jim ❖ Once your seedlings emerge from the soil, reduce the heat! Warm soil is a seed's best friend, but a seedling's worst enemy. Be sure your flats continue to get plenty of light, however.

Stretched seedlings tend to flop over because their spindly stems can't support the weight of the leaves. They're also more vulnerable to disease. You may spot a few dead seedlings in one spot, and watch in horror as that one spot becomes a slowly widening circle. This means that damping-off disease has set in. You'll have to discard your plants and soil, wash and sterilize your flats and tools, and try, try again.

I often illustrate plant diseases using a simple triangle. A plant will fall prey to a disease only if three conditions exist at the same time:

- the organism that causes the disease must be present.
- the plant must be susceptible to that particular disease.
- the environment must be right for infection (for example, some fungi thrive when there's lots of humidity).

If you can eliminate even one corner of this triangle, infection cannot occur.

Pansy 'Contessa Mix'

Direct seeding in the garden

What is "direct seeding"?
What annuals are best for this?

Lois ❖ When you direct seed, you sow directly into your garden—no transplanting required. This works best for cool-season plants that mature quickly and tolerate cool soil.

Jim ❖ The problem with direct seeding in our climate is that most annuals take too long to flower. We sow our pansies inside the greenhouses in early February, and then transplant them outside in April when they're already in bloom. If we seeded those same pansies directly into the garden, we wouldn't see any blooms before the end of July!

If you're going to direct seed some of your bedding plants, choose your varieties carefully.

If I plant my seeds today and it gets cold tonight, will they freeze?

Lois ❖ Once your seeds are tucked into bed, they can make it through some pretty cold nights. Even the lightest covering of soil will provide more than enough insulation for your seeds.

Jim ❖ If you're unlucky enough to plant at the beginning of a long cold, damp spell, some of your seeds may rot before they have a chance to germinate. However, the occasional touch of frost is nothing to worry about.

What annuals tend to self-sow?
Does this classify them as a perennials?

Lois ❖ Violas, pansies, calendula, bachelor's buttons, and cosmos self-sow like crazy, especially the pansies! But even though they self-sow, however, all of these plants are considered annuals, because they complete their life cycle in one season.

Jim ❖ Certain annuals self-seed more than others because they have a shorter life cycle. In northern climates, many annual bedding plants simply don't have time to develop mature seeds.

Can an ice plant (*mesembryanthemum*) seed itself for next year?

Lois ❖ I consider it highly unlikely. Ice plant seeds require a long growing season to develop.

I have pansies growing in my garden where I didn't plant them. Why?

Lois ❖ The pansies you planted in the spring probably produced lots of wonderful flowers—and lots of seeds. These got released by the plants, settled into your soil, and made a surprise appearance the following spring! The year before last, I planted several clumps of Ball's Bingo Pansies, and this spring hundreds of tiny plants emerged in my flower bed.

Jim ❖ Chances are, these "surprise" pansies showed up in the late spring or early summer, since they didn't have the same early start as transplanted pansies.

Should I soak my sweet pea seeds before planting them?

Lois ❖ Don't soak your sweet pea seeds! There's no advantage to doing this. Simply place them about 2 cm deep into the soil and water, water, water. And don't forget the inoculant!

Jim ❖ Soaking your seeds can literally drown them. Seeds require oxygen to grow, and they cannot get enough when they're underwater. Also, if the soaked seeds dry out in the ground before they emerge and develop roots, they will die. Finally, if the seeds soak up too much water, they stand a much greater chance of rotting in the soil.

Can I grow lavatera from seed?

Lois ❖ Yes, lavatera grows wonderfully from seed. You can even direct seed it in your garden.

Jim ❖ Lavatera has a tendency to grow rapidly from seed . It's very prone to root-rot diseases, however, and should be treated soon after the seedlings emerge. You can apply a fungicide treatment of benomyl and Truban (etridiazole), but be careful with the Truban, as it's easy to overdose!

If you're starting your seeds indoors, it's particularly important to cool the soil temperature to 16°C as soon as the seedlings emerge, because lavatera grows so rapidly.

My garden is sprinkled with poppies from last year, and I'd like to make sure it doesn't happen again.

Lois ❖ Poppies certainly are prolific! To prevent volunteer poppies, simply make sure your poppies don't get the chance to produce seeds. Pick off the large seed pods before they ripen and burst. It's an easy job that my grandkids love to do. Many poppies produce attractive seed pods, so you may want to save them as a decoration.

When is it too late to direct seed?

Lois ❖ The question shouldn't be when is it too late, but rather when is it too early to seed plants outside. Far too many people miss the boat by waiting too long to plant! Take a little risk and plant early. That way, you'll be able to enjoy your bedding plants for much longer.

Jim ❖ Read the seed packets to see how long it will take for your plants to grow to maturity. If the maturity date will coincide with the average first fall-frost date in your area, you are running the risk that you'll lose your plants. If you've missed your chance to direct seed in the early spring, go out and buy bedding plants. Otherwise, you'll spend weeks waiting for those first blooms, when you could be enjoying a lush, colourful garden.

Petunia 'Celebrity Chiffon Morn'

Cuttings

What's the best method for taking and rooting cuttings?

Lois ❖ Take lots, and take them from different parts of the plant. Note which part of the plant roots best—it'll save you a lot of trouble next time. I like to take cuttings in the morning, when the plant is firm and less stressed. Remember to let the cut ends dry just a bit before transplanting, and keep your cuttings in a cool, shady spot until you're ready to plant! As for rooting your cuttings, you're best off to keep trying different methods until you find one that suits you best.

Jim ❖ Not all cuttings root easily. Herbaceous cuttings, such as geraniums or nasturtiums, usually root much more quickly and reliably than hardwood cuttings taken from trees and shrubs. Cuttings from the newer (but not newest) growth on a plant will generally root better than that from older growth (mandevilla is one exception to this). Rooting hormones are very helpful on woody cuttings, although they don't make as much difference on softer cuttings. When rooting your cuttings, watch your polarity—in other words, don't plant the cuttings upside down. As silly as this sounds, it's very easy to do!

What is the optimum temperature to root cuttings?

Lois ❖ 20° to 22°C is ideal—day and night—until your cuttings have rooted. Be careful to watch the temperature—cuttings can be fussy!

Jim ❖ Temperature is crucial. If the soil is too cold, the cuttings will rot. On the other hand, too much heat will inhibit rooting and dry the cuttings out. The temperature should not fall below 18°C or rise above 26°C.

Don't go by air temperature! The soil can be much cooler than the room's air temperature, due to evaporation. Monitor the soil temperature with a probe, and keep it within the correct range using heat cables.

How many days will my cuttings take to root?

Lois ❖ This question doesn't really have one specific answer. Top-quality cuttings, under ideal conditions in a greenhouse, generally root in 2 to 3 weeks. If the cuttings are of a lower quality, or if the rooting conditions are less than optimal, it takes longer.

Of course, there are always exceptions! For example, mandevilla cuttings take over a month to root, even under ideal conditions.

Should I use rooting compounds for my cuttings?

Lois ❖ It all depends on the cutting. I never use them to root my geraniums, nasturtiums, or impatiens, and they all turn out wonderfully. However, many people do find that rooting compounds help them successfully root their cuttings.

Jim ❖ Rooting compounds imitate a naturally occurring compound called auxin, found in the growing tips of plants. Auxin is required to initiate root growth on stems.

Rooting compounds are effective if used in the right amount. Use too little, and you might as well not use any. Too much, and you'll actually inhibit rooting. To avoid an overdose, tap off any excess compound after you dip the cuttings. Alternatively, you can lightly dust the cuttings with the compound rather than dipping them. Use a duster bottle, such as a talcum powder container. I prefer this method, because it reduces the risk of spreading disease.

Petunia 'Cascadia Charlie'

Do you grow mandevilla from seeds or cuttings?

Lois ❖ We always grow our mandevilla from cuttings.

Jim ❖ You can't buy mandevilla seed. It is only vegetatively propagated. Mandevilla roots best when the cutting is taken from the third or fourth branch below the tip of the shoot.

Fuchsia 'Dark Eyes'

How do I propagate geraniums from cuttings?

Lois ❖ First and foremost, start with a nice, healthy mother (stock) plant. This is essential—if the stock plant is diseased, the infection can spread to all the cuttings. Often, you can purchase cuttings from a greenhouse, which saves you the trouble of keeping a stock plant over the winter.
My best tip to you is to take double the amount of cuttings that you'll need, because chances are a lot of them won't survive. Believe me—I've learned this the hard way!

Jim ❖ The key to propagating geraniums is to start in early January with a healthy stock plant. That way, you'll be able to take cuttings by late January and early February.

Grower's
edge

Propagating geraniums and fuchsias

• Remember to wash your hands before handling the cuttings. Diseases can be spread from such common plant material as lettuce and tobacco.

• Use 5 cm-long cuttings (terminals/new shoots), as bigger cuttings tend to fall over and not root as well. Let cuttings dry for 1–2 hours prior to planting, to prevent the development of disease on moist stem ends.

• Trim lower leaves, then stick cuttings into peat pellets or oasis cubes (available at your garden centre). Peat pellets are a better choice for home gardeners, because they remain moist longer. Be careful not to crowd your cuttings!

• Water the cubes or pellets and mist the foliage.

• Place a tent of plastic over the cuttings to retain moisture.

• Check the root temperature often with a temperature probe. Keep it near 22°C, to prevent the cuttings from rotting or drying out.

• Keep the cuttings in bright light but avoid direct sunlight, which can cause the air inside the tent to overheat.

• Fertilize once the roots have become 1 to 2 cm long.

• About three weeks after you take your cuttings, they should be ready to transplant.

Transplanting

Lois, you've always said, "Plant early!" Isn't this risky in a cold country like Canada?

Lois ❖ Not at all! Many people wait far too long to plant, under the mistaken impression that even a touch of frost will wipe out all of their bedding plants. A degree or two of frost will have little or no effect on many transplants. If a frost threatens, you can always cover some of the tender varieties. It's a risk worth taking, once you consider the payoff. While your more cautious neighbours are still waiting for their first blooms, you'll have a garden bursting in colour!

Jim ❖ Here at Hole's, we always place our flats of pansies outside in mid-April. It doesn't matter if it snows or freezes; as long as the pansies have been acclimatized, they can take it! We do cover them on cold nights, though, to prevent frost marks on the leaves.

While it's true that pansies are tougher than most annuals, there's no reason to wait until late in the spring to put out your bedding plants. Once you hit your average last spring frost date (May 6 in our area), you should have most of your cool-season bedding plants in the ground. Shade-loving plants such as begonias and impatiens tend to be more sensitive to cool temperatures, so plant them a few weeks later.

Are there any disadvantages to planting early?

Lois ❖ People who wait until later in the season can eliminate most of their weeds before transplanting. When they cultivate their flowerbeds in late May, they destroy the weeds that sprouted in the early spring. Those who plant early have to remove those weeds by hand from between their annuals.

Of course, there's another way of looking at it. Those weeds don't wait around until the end of May before getting busy in your garden, so why should you?

Jim ❖ Some of your more delicate bedding plants don't grow as well when the soil and air are still cool. You should let things warm up a bit before planting zinnias and coleus, for example. Still, the fact remains that most people wait longer than they should before planting. The advantages of planting early far outweigh the disadvantages.

I've heard that you have to "harden off" seedlings before you plant them outside. How do I do this?

Lois ❖ Just as it takes some time for us to adjust to the morning chill after spending a luxurious amount of time in the shower, seedlings find it a bit of a shock to make the transition from the greenhouse to the garden. All of a sudden, they're hit with intense sunlight, wind, and cold night temperatures. When you harden your bedding plants off, you give them a chance to gradually adjust to outdoor conditions.

Jim ❖ To harden off seedlings, simply move the pots or packs to a bright (but not directly sunlit) location outdoors at least a week prior to planting. Be careful not to let your seedlings dry out, and protect them from high winds or severe cold. Bring them indoors if there's a risk of frost, or else cover them with an old sheet, towel, blanket, newspaper, or cardboard box.

Do I have to harden off my purchased bedding plants, or only the ones I grow myself?

Lois ❖ Some greenhouses sell plants that have already been hardened off, but this requires a lot of labour and space. If you're not sure, ask. Of course, if you're buying plants after the May long weekend, hardening off is not an issue.

Jim ❖ Many greenhouses do harden off their plants before selling them. We grow our pansies, snapdragons, and many other annuals outside for weeks. As our other bedding plants mature, we lower the temperature in our greenhouses to "toughen them" or "harden them off."

When transplanting seedlings, is it best to do it when they are very small or wait until they've grown a bit larger?

Lois ❖ Unless it's still very cold outside, there's no reason to postpone transplanting your seedlings. The best time to transplant is after the first true leaves have emerged. This tells you that your seedling has rooted well and won't experience much transplant shock.

Jim ❖ The very first leaves on a seedling, the cotyledon leaves (commonly called the "seed" leaves), don't resemble the "true" leaves of a mature plant. Transplant after the first true leaves appear and before your plant outgrows its container.

What is "transplant shock" and how do I prevent it?

Lois ❖ Every plant is traumatized to a certain extent at transplanting. This "transplant shock" may cause your plant to stop growing for a period—in fact, it might even appear to shrink!

The cure is water. After transplanting, immediately apply 10-52-10 fertilizer. Do this, and your plants will make the transition without skipping a beat.

How cold does it have to get before my plants will freeze? Are plants more vulnerable in the spring or in the fall?

Lois ❖ The amount of cold a plant can withstand depends more on the variety than on the season. At our greenhouse, some of our plants have endured freezing temperatures with very little damage:

Violas and Pansies to -10°C, Godetia to -9°C, Snapdragons to -5°C, Dianthus to -5°C, Petunias -3°C, Geraniums to -3°C.
Most cool season plants are pretty tough. Often, the frost just damages the softest growth (the new growth), and the plants recover fully in a week or so. In fact, frost can serve the same effect as pinching the growing tip, resulting in more branching and a bushier, fuller plant. Have patience.

Jim ❖ Your plants' vulnerablility to frost isn't so much a question of spring or fall, but of the age of the tissue. Young, soft tissue has the highest water content, and therefore suffers the first and most severe frost damage. Given a few weeks of milder weather, most of your plants will recover from a light frost.

Often, the roots of my bedding plants have grown through the bottom of the plastic pack. Will the plants be damaged when I transplant them?

Lois ❖ Your plants will be fine. Rip away any roots growing through the bottom of the pack, and loosen up the root ball before planting. This encourages your plant to spread its roots into the soil more rapidly.

Jim ❖ The roots that come out of the bottom of your pack and the roots winding around inside the pack are fine: they won't inhibit the flower's growth. However, if the roots are very dense and clustered together, you must gently pull them apart before transplanting. Otherwise, the roots won't spread beyond the small space they had in the pack.

My plants are all stretched out in the packs. Should I cut them back before I transplant?

Lois ❖ Avoid buying tall, spindly-looking plants, even if the price seems irresistible. There's really nothing you can do to salvage them. They will grow, but they will never do as well as they should. Buy only healthy, well-branched vigorous plants, and get them into the ground before they have a chance to outgrow their containers.

Jim ❖ When they're weak, tall and spindly to begin with, plants don't recover well after you cut them back. If you cut too far into the old growth, new growth will be very slow to emerge. Spindly plants are also more vulnerable to damage from insects and disease.

What is the best fertilizer to use when transplanting plants?

Lois ❖ 10-52-10 is the best all-purpose fertilizer to get your garden started. Before transplanting, moisten the bed with plain water. Then, immediately after transplanting, soak the bed thoroughly with your fertilizer solution.

One of my favorite times to plant is a day or two after a good rain, when the soil is naturally moist and soft.

Jim ❖ 10-52-10 is the best choice. When you transplant, you want fast, vigourous root development. The high level of phosphorus (the middle number) encourages this. Nitrogen (the first number) promotes leafy growth. This fertilizer is lower in nitrogen, because you'd prefer your plant to devote its energy to root development.

Fertilize well at transplanting, and once a week thereafter with 10-52-10 (5mL/litre) once per week. After two weeks, switch to a good all-purpose (20-20-20) fertilizer.

I've kept my bedding plants in my garage, and they've started to turn yellow. Have I done something wrong?

Lois ❖ You're not the first person to learn this lesson the hard way. In fact, the staff in our retail bedding-plant greenhouse refer to this condition as "garage-plant syndrome."

Don't leave your plants in the garage! Put them into the ground as soon as you've had a chance to harden them off. If you can't plant them right away, make sure to put them outside during the day, and only put them back in the garage at night if it's going to be cold. Inside a garage, even near a window, plants don't receive nearly enough light to maintain healthy growth.

Jim ❖ Outside, even on a cloudy day, your plants receive at least twice as much light as they do indoors in front of a bright, south-facing window. At the same time, the outdoor conditions help prepare them for transplanting. Keeping your plants out of the garage is just as important as keeping your car out of the garden!

Intensity (fc) of different light sources

Light Source	Location	fc (foot candle*)
Sunlight	outdoors - full sun	10,000
	greenhouse - winter overcast	1,000
	home indoors:	
	1 ft from north window	200 -500
	3 ft from north window	100 - 180
	1 ft from south window - shade	500 - 900
	1 ft from east window	250 - 400
	2 ft from east or west window	150 - 250

* Foot candles is a unit of measurement that is rapidly becoming obsolete in the greenhouse industry. The new term is micromoles per square metre per second and is abbreviated $\mu mol/m^{-2}/s^{-1}$. The approximate conversion to fc is to divide foot candles by 5 to get micromoles.

Frost Protection

What happens when a plant freezes?

Lois ❖ Like humans, plants can get frostbite. If the damage isn't too extensive, the plant will recover.

Jim ❖ When a plant is hit by frost, the water within the cells freezes. The cell walls burst, and the tissue rapidly dehydrates and dies.

Why are some plants more vulnerable to frost than others?

Jim ❖ Some plants are adapted at a cellular level to survive frost. The tissue contains water both within and between the individual cells. The water inside the cell walls contains more sugars and salts than the water outside. The salts lower the freezing point inside the cell (much in the same way that salt melts ice on your driveway). As long as the water inside the cell doesn't freeze and form crystals, the cell will remain intact.

Plants native to tropical regions, such as marigolds, didn't need this protection against frost and so never developed it. Others, such as today's hardy pansies, have evolved to withstand the fluctuating temperatures of a northern spring.

If I cover my plants at night, won't the cover crush the plants?

Lois ❖ No. Plants are stronger than you think! The weight of fabric distributed over all the plants won't harm them.

That's not to say that you should toss a heavy quilt over your marigolds! Lightweight fabrics like burlap, sheets or light blankets provide all the protection your plants need.

Gazania 'Daybreak Red Stripe'

Can I cover my plants with sheets of plastic or plastic buckets? I don't want my good cotton sheets to get dirty.

Lois ❖ Chances are, your sheets won't get anything on them that doesn't come out in the wash. However, if you're worried about your good sheets, keep them out of the garden! Dig some old sheets out of the closet, or grab some towels or burlap sacking. Don't use plastic, though, because it provides no insulation. Most garden centres sell a frost blanket which is durable and easy to use, stores well and offers excellent protection to your plants.

Jim ❖ Plastic buckets provide some insulation, but they're not as effective as plain old fabric. Plastic sheets provide no insulation at all. They're only useful if attached to the foundation of your house and draped over your plants. This traps some of the heat from your house. However, light fabric is still your simplest and most effective option.

Frost blankets offer excellent protection.

Miscellaneous

What is the difference between fibrous roots and tuberous roots?

Lois ❖ Like the name implies, fibrous roots are thin, fibre-like roots branching out from a central stem. A tuberous root, on the other hand, is a thicker, fleshy underground growth, like on a potato or dahlia. Tuberous roots also form fibrous-branching roots. A good example of this would be a begonia.

Jim ❖ Tuberous roots form during the late summer, collecting and storing plant nutrients for regrowth the following spring. For instance, tuberous begonias start from seed. By midsummer, the large plant has fibrous roots. As the days begin to shorten, the begonia produces tubers in preparation for the approaching winter.

What is a vegetative plant?

Lois ❖ Vegetative plants are produced from cuttings, not from seeds.

Jim ❖ "Vegetative" refers to how the plant is propagated. Remove cuttings (usually branches) from the stock or mother plant (see the earlier question on geraniums). Root these cuttings, and transplant them into pots. Because the cuttings come directly from the mother plant, parent and offspring are genetically identical.

We propagate plants vegetatively for two main reasons. Some varieties produce little or no viable seed, so vegetative propagation is the only way to produce more plants. Other varieties, especially hybrids, produce variable seed. By taking cuttings, we can produce plants that will grow to be identical to the parents.

Petunia 'Tidal Wave Cherry'

Petunia 'Misty Lilac Wave'

What do bedding plants need to grow well?

Lois ❖ Plants need water, sunlight, good soil, carbon dioxide, and fertilizer. You'd be surprised how many people forget to water and don't bother to fertilize. And for gosh sakes, if you have a shady area, plant only shade-tolerant species.

Jim ❖ In addition to what Mom has said, all plants require fairly large quantities of three basic nutrients: nitrogen, phosphorus, and potassium (represented by the elemental symbols N for nitrogen, P for phosphorus, and K for potassium). During initial growth, most plants need extra phosphorus to help them establish roots: 10-52-10 fertilizer is ideal. Later, an all-purpose fertilizer such as 20-20-20 will provide a good balance of all three nutrients.

Watering

How much water do plants require during a season?

Lois ❖ Lots! Bedding plants tend to be thirsty. You're more likely to kill them by underwatering than overwatering.

Jim ❖ Mom's right, though there are exceptions to this rule. Watering annuals can be just a bit tricky, because precipitation varies every season and each species has different water requirements. Several main factors determine the amount of water your plants need:

- The type of plant. Certain plants need more water than others.

- Air temperature. You have to water more often during hot weather.

- Humidity. When the humidity's high, plants and soil lose less moisture to evaporation. Therefore, you don't need to water as often.

- Soil type. If your soil is rich in organic material, it does a better job of absorbing and holding moisture. This also cuts down your need to water. The sandier your soil, the quicker it dries.

Do hanging baskets need extra water?

Lois ❖ On a hot day, if you water a hanging basket in the morning, it may be dry when you come home from work. The smaller the pot, the greater the problem. That's why I tell people not to bother with hanging baskets smaller than 35 cm in diameter. One trick I like to use when my hanging basket accidentally becomes too dry and the soil has shrunk from the sides of the pot is to submerge the entire basket in a pail of water until the soil is fully soaked.

Jim ❖ Hanging baskets tend to be more exposed to the wind and sun, so they're particularly vulnerable to evaporation. At the same time, they can't draw any extra moisture from the surrounding area. Your plants are dependent on the moisture in the container which only you can provide.

A hanging basket that is fully grown tends to shed overhead water. Therefore watering at the soil level is essential to prevent drying.

I've heard that I should be careful when watering on sunny days, because water on the leaves can cause burning. Is this true?

Lois ❖ There's no truth at all to this popular myth. Water on leaves can, however, foster various diseases. Grey mould, for example, thrives on moist foliage. This is why I always recommend watering with a good flood nozzle, so that you can send all of the water to the soil around the base of the plant where it's needed.

Jim ❖ It sounds like you've heard the well-established myth that water droplets act as miniature lenses that magnify light and cause the foliage to burn. Don't believe it!
Look at it this way: what would happen if water droplets really did burn leaves? A brief rainstorm followed by sunshine would burn every plant for miles around!

That said, it's still not a good idea to water during the heat of the day, because you lose too much moisture to evaporation. Water your garden first thing in the morning, to give your soil a chance to absorb as much of the water as possible.

Moisture holding capacities

Soil Texture	Max amount of water soil can hold Weight (%)
Sandy	6
Sandy Loam	14
Loam	22
Clay Loam	27
Silty Loam	31
Clay	35

ie. 100 kg of sandy soil can hold 6 kg of water when the soil is completely saturated.

When I water my containers, how do I know if they've been watered enough? Should the water be dripping out of the bottom?

Lois ❖ You've got to thoroughly soak the container each and every time. Don't just "baptize" your plants! Sprinkling a bit of water on the surface will result in shallow, under-developed roots. You want the moisture to go right to the bottom. I like to water until I see water flowing from the bottom of the pot.

Jim ❖ Water your containers every time the soil surface begins to dry out. Assuming you have good potting soil, it's nearly impossible to overwater. Properly balanced soil retains the right amount of moisture, and allows any excess to drain away. If your soil doesn't stay wet at all or if it becomes waterlogged, you should amend it.

Over the years, it has been customers who under-water garden plants that have experienced the most problems—rarely is overwatering unto itself an issue.

If I know a plant is drought tolerant, should I bother watering it?

Lois ❖ Remember what tolerant means. Just because a plant can withstand drought doesn't mean that it thrives in drought! Without water, even the toughest plants eventually give up the ghost. The most important thing to remember is to water your plants regularly until they are well established, even the drought-tolerant ones.

Jim ❖ Drought-tolerant plants don't like being wet all the time, so it's a good idea to allow the surface of the soil to dry out between waterings. Provided you get a good, soaking rain every week or so, you might get away without watering your drought-tolerant plants. However, they definitely need your help during extended dry spells.

I can't keep my flower beds moist enough. What should I do?

Lois ❖ Get a proper flood nozzle and soak that soil thoroughly. A trigger nozzle is a poor choice; it waters with a harsh narrow spray which doesn't allow the moisture to soak into the soil. A flood nozzle waters with a heavy, soft flow which provides lots of water to the plants..

Jim ❖ In addition to watering properly, add organic material—peat moss, rich loam, manure, and compost—to help your soil retain moisture. Stay away from sand. If you find you still can't keep up with the watering, consider installing an automated drip system.

Drip-Irrigation Systems

This handy garden gadget can drastically reduce your workload and your water bill. Drip irrigation distributes water to your plants very efficiently, one drop at a time.

This is not new technology, but it is much more common in large-scale operations. In our greenhouse, we use hundreds of metres of drip tubes to irrigate crops like hanging baskets and geraniums. Now, drip irrigation is also catching on with home gardeners.

The system consists of lengths of thin plastic pipe fitted with special emitters at regular intervals—every 30 cm or so. Each emitter is a tiny plastic labyrinth that slows and equalizes water flow, to ensure that each emitter drips out water at the same rate.

Because drip irrigation delivers moisture directly to the soil, you lose less moisture to evaporation. None of the water is sprayed into the air or onto the foliage, as is the case with overhead sprinklers. Over time, you save a lot of water.

As the water drips out of the emitters, it seeps down into the soil and spreads horizontally. The system doesn't work well for seedlings, since their roots are too small to reach the moisture. For well-established plants, however, drip irrigation maintains a consistent supply of moisture along the entire length of pipe.

Drip-irrigation systems are relatively inexpensive and easy to use. The pipe is surprisingly lightweight—you can easily pick up a 150 m roll with one hand.

You can easily create your own system, even if you're not mechanically inclined. Let's say you have a garden, 6 metres by 6 metres, with 10 rows of annuals. First, lay one 6 m length of drip irrigation pipe along each row. Clamp each pipe shut at one end and leave it open at the other. Next, using simple plastic connectors, hook the open ends of the pipes into a central supply pipe. Finally, simply hook it into your outside tap, and turn on the water. Voila—you're on your way to conserving hundreds of litres of water a year.

This system works best if you plant your garden in rows, rather than in mass plantings. One tip: let the coiled tube warm up in the sun before you begin. This will make it soft, pliable, and easy to work with.

Install your drip tubing early, before your plants become too dense. You'll need enough room to slide the tubing between them.

Attach a relatively inexpensive water timer between the faucet and the drip tubing. This will allow you to set the time, frequency and length of your irrigation. With a bit of research and experimentation, you'll soon determine exactly how much water your plants need.

In the fall, simply pull up the hoses, pull off the connectors, and store your system until spring.

Fertilizer

Which works better, chemical or organic fertilizer?

Lois ❖ Both work equally well. As long as your plants get the nutrients they need, they don't really care how they get them. I like to use water soluble fertilizers because they act so quickly and they are so easy to use, but many people achieve excellent results with fish fertilizers, kelp meal, manure teas, and even bat guano.

Jim ❖ All fertilizers are actually "chemical" fertilizers, in that they deliver the same elements and compounds to your plants. However, organic and non-organic fertilizers differ in the way they deliver these nutrients.

When you add manure to your soil, for example, microorganisms in the soil digest it, breaking it down into separate compounds such as ammonium, nitrates, phosphates, and iron oxides. Chemical fertilizers, such as 20-20-20, also contain ammonium, iron, phosphates, and so on. Unlike organic fertilizers, however, they don't have to be broken down before releasing nutrients to the plant. In either case, the plant eventually absorbs the same compounds in the same form, whether it's from an organic or non-organic source.

Keep in mind, however, that organic fertilizers provide more than short-term benefit to your plants. Because they take time to break down, they provide a long-term reservoir of nutrients in your soil. They also improve your soil's texture and moisture retention. The organic fertilizers generally have a low analysis (i.e., fish fertilizer is approximately 3-1-1), so you need larger quantities to provide the same amounts of nutrients as a chemical fertilizer.

Organic Fertilizer: Manure

Why do gardeners add manure to their soil?

Lois ❖ Manure adds organic material to your soil. Make sure you use well-rotted manure, not fresh. Fresh manure will burn your plants.

Jim ❖ Manure builds up the organic matter in the soil. It absorbs and retains nutrients and water, and provides a slow-release source of nutrients while greatly improving soil texture.

Does it matter what kind of manure I use (sheep, steer, etc.)?

Lois ❖ By and large, manure is manure! It doesn't differ much from animal to animal.

Jim ❖ Just remember to use well-composted manure, which is more decomposed than fresh. If you're using mushroom manure (usually horse manure that has been used for mushroom culture), be careful not to add too much. It contains very high levels of salts and can burn burn your plants. Don't add more than a 1-cm layer of mushroom manure, and be sure to mix it thoroughly into your soil.

What is manure tea?

Lois ❖ I've never made manure tea, or compost tea, but a lot of people swear by it. Like the name suggests, it's a liquid fertilizer made by soaking manure or compost in water.

You brew it in much the same way as you would Orange Pekoe, but in a bigger pot! Just shovel some manure or compost into a burlap bag and tie it shut. Then immerse your "tea bag" into a large bucket or barrel of water, cover it, and leave it to steep for a few days. Before using the liquid on your plants, be sure to dilute it to a very light brown colour.
Use the tea in place of regular water. In my opinion, the amount of work in brewing this tea far outweighs the benefit to the plants, but don't let me stop you from giving it a try. I wouldn't use it on edible flowers, however, in case of disease.

Jim ❖ Keep a few things in mind when using manure or compost tea:

- Manure may contain plant diseases, and seedlings are especially susceptible.

- Manure teas may contain high levels of ammonia that can injure seedlings.

- Because tea is a weakened solution of manure, it may not contain enough nutrients for rapidly growing plants. Also, as with any manure, the composition will vary depending on age and origin of the manure.

Typical Composition of Manures

Source	Dry Matter (%)	Approximate Composition (% dry weight)		
		N	P_2O_5	K_2O
Dairy	15–25	0.6–2.1	0.7–1.1	2.4–3.6
Feedlot	20–40	1.0–2.5	0.9–1.6	2.4–3.6
Horse	15–25	1.7–3.0	0.7–1.2	1.2–2.2
Poultry	20–30	2.0–4.5	4.5–6.0	1.2–2.4
Sheep	25–35	3.0–4.0	1.2–1.6	3.0–4.0
Swine	20–30	3.0–4.0	0.4–0.6	0.5–1.0

Chemical Fertilizer: Composition

On fertilizer packages, what do the three numbers represent?

Lois ❖ The numbers refer to the percentage by weight of nitrogen—phosphate—potash in the fertilizer.

Jim ❖ Nitrogen is crucial for leaf growth, phosphates promote strong root development, and potash aids in all-round plant health.

Do brand names matter, or is one 20-20-20 fertilizer like the next?

Jim ❖ The numbers represent a minimum chemical analysis; no reputable company would try to shortchange you. The only differences might lie in the ease with which the fertilizer dissolves, the chemical formulation of each nutrient, and the composition of its inert ingredients. In general, though, you'll find that most 20-20-20 fertilizers work well in the garden.

Petunia 'Cascadia Yellow with Eye'

Using Fertilizer In The Garden

Will I hurt my plants if I continue to use 10-52-10 after 3 weeks?

Lois ❖ You won't harm your plants, but you won't give them the proper balance of nutrients. Once your new transplants have had a few weeks to become established, you should always switch to 20-20-20 or a comparable fertilizer.

Jim ❖ 10-52-10, or starter fertilizer, simply doesn't address all your plants' needs for the entire season. Once the roots have become established, your plants need a better balance of nitrogen and potassium in order to help them grow properly. If you continue to use 10-52-10, the plant will still look healthy, but it won't reach its full potential.

Do I dilute fertilizer? How?

Lois ❖ About 5 ml per litre works well with an all-purpose fertilizer (20-20-20). Just add the fertilizer before filling your watering can. Or you might find it simpler to do what I do. Every time I water, I add a good pinch of fertilizer to my two-gallon can.

Jim ❖ Professional growers base their fertilizer program on "parts per million of nitrogen." With 20-20-20, for example, a typical feed rate would be about 200 parts per million (ppm) of nitrogen. This works out to 1 g of 20-20-20 soluble fertilizer per 1 litre of water.
• 1 g/litre of 20-20-20 = 200 ppm
• 2 g/litre of 20-20-20 = 400 ppm
• 0.5 g/litre of 20-20-20 = 100 ppm
For seedlings, 50 to 100 ppm of 10-52-10 works well (0.5 to 1 g/litre). Once seedlings emerge, increase the amount to 100 to 200 ppm (0.5 to 1 g/litre of 20-20-20). For regular bedding plants (in hanging baskets, beds, or planter boxes), 200 ppm of 20-20-20 works best (1 g/litre). If you're fertilizing once a week, use 400 ppm of fertilizer (2 g/litre).

Why doesn't my granular fertilizer dissolve?

Lois ❖ Some fertilizers are meant to be dissolved very slowly. They're deliberately formulated to dissolve gradually once they're added to the soil.

Jim ❖ Unless the package specifically says "water soluble," assume that the granular fertilizer is not readily soluble. Granular fertilizers should be worked into the soil.

Portulaca 'Yubi Rose'

My plants need oxygen.
Can I get liquid fertilizer with oxygen?

Lois ❖ You can. Some liquid fertilizers purportedly contain oxygen. I'm not convinced, though, that it's any better than regular fertilizer.

Jim ❖ Oxygen is not something you "inject" into the soil. If the soil is nice and loose, oxygen will infiltrate easily. No "oxygen" fertilizer can provide the one crucial ingredient that all good soils require—pore space.

Do sunflowers leach all the nutrients from the soil?
My plants near the sunflowers are very small while
the same plants further away are big and beautiful.

Lois ❖ Those big, bright sunflowers can overshadow the other plants in your garden–in more ways than one! Because they're so large and showy, they make nearby plants seem less impressive. At the same time, they literally overshadow smaller plants, blotting out the sun. You're best off giving sunflowers a space of their own.

Jim ❖ A fully grown sunflower absorbs seventeen times more water than a human per day. Because of this, they tend to rob valuable moisture from nearby plants. Sunflowers also consume a lot of nutrients. In particular, they need extra potassium to develop their stem structures.

Because of their sheer size, sunflowers tie up a lot of valuable nutrients. At the end of the season, composting sunflowers returns not only the nutrients to the soil, but also a good supply of organic matter.

Deadheading

Why do I need to deadhead?

Lois ❖ Deadheading is like housecleaning: it's important to stay on top of it if you want to keep your garden looking neat and clean. Removing faded flowers also encourages your plants to continue blooming and producing new growth. It's well worth the few minutes it takes!

Jim ❖ Once a flower fades, the plant begins putting a lot of energy into seed production. If you remove the flower before the seeds form, the plant will divert that energy into new flowers and foliage. Dead flowers also encourage disease when they land on other flowers or foliage.

How do I deadhead?

Lois ❖ Get out into your garden in the morning once the dew has dried. Flower heads snap off more easily when the plants are nice and cool. On geraniums and snapdragons, it's okay to leave the penduncle (the stem that supports the flower) on.

Jim ❖ Deadheading is quite easy. Just snap or cut off the flower heads as soon as they begin to deteriorate. For most plants, simply snap or pinch the stem right below the flower head.

Pinching back encourages many plants to branch out more.

What does self-cleaning mean?

Lois ❖ Self-cleaning means that no deadheading is required–the plant cleans up after itself. The dead blooms simply fall away from the plant. Impatiens are a pefect example of this, and the new petunia varieties like Madness or Wave are great for this too.

Jim ❖ On self-cleaning plants, the flower drops cleanly from the plant, without clinging. Because the flowers on self-cleaning plants often don't set seed, the only debris they leave behind are dried-up petals, which are hardly noticeable.

What is pinching back? Do I need to do it? How much of it should I do?

Lois ❖ Pinching back is when you remove the tip of the plant (the terminal growth). This encourages the plant to branch out more, becoming fuller and bushier. Most plants deserve a good pinch—but not too hard! If you can't do it easily with your fingers, use scissors. For example, scissors work best for petunias and snapdragons, but your fingers will do for marigolds.

Jim ❖ Pinching increases branching and flowering. The shoot tips of your plants contain concentrated levels of hormones called auxins.

Auxins inhibit bud growth. The closer the buds are to the tip, the smaller they tend to be. This gives the plant a "Christmas tree" shape. Once you pinch off the tip, the buds are less inhibited and are free to grow vigorously.

Weeding

Can I use weed barrier with my annuals?

Lois ❖ You certainly can, but I'll warn you that the fabric must must be cut extensively to allow bedding plants to grow through; this limits its effectiveness from year to year. I would rather use other covers like bark mulch. You might be better off in the long run to get down into the dirt and pull those weeds the old-fashioned way!

Jim ❖ Be careful your weed barrier does not prevent moisture from penetrating to the root zone. Never use plastic. Commercial weed barriers are a woven fabric.

What's the easiest way to pull weeds?

Lois ❖ If you weed a few days after a good rain, the weeds pull out of the soil more easily. It is much easier weeding after a rainfall than when the soil is dry. If you do find yourself weeding a dry bed, use a sturdy hoe to get around the leaves of the weed, and pull it up from its base. Be sure to add compost or peatmoss every year to keep the soil soft and easy to weed.

How do I get rid of weed seeds in my soil?

Lois ❖ Always, always plant into clean soil (if at all possible)! If it takes one or even two years to get rid of problem weeds, do it. It's worth the effort!

To eliminate a severe weed problem from your garden, keep it bare all summer. Rototill, hoe, or spray for weeds when necessary. It's hard work, but it's the only way you'll be able to reduce your weed problem in the long run.

If you insist on planting a garden, try dividing your problem area in half. Plant one half of your garden, and treat the other half for weeds. Next year, switch sides—think of it like summer fallow. In the planted section, you must be very careful not to allow any weeds to go to seed to prevent more weed problems the following season!

Jim ❖ Here are my best tips for reducing your weed problem.

• Never allow the weeds to go to seed. A single pigweed can produce up to one million seeds each year!
• Perennial weeds that spread by rhizomes, such as quackgrass, require a rigorous, regular tillage program. You may have to till the soil six times a year to get rid of these persistent weeds. The best solution is to apply the herbicide glyphosate when the perennial weeds are 15 to 20 cm tall.
• Don't introduce weeds into your garden in the first place—always buy clean potting or garden soils.
• Never plant into areas infested with tough-to-control weeds like thistle or quack grass—eliminate these weeds first.

Doesn't rototilling damage the texture of the soil?

Lois ❖ Rototilling won't destroy your soil, as long as you're careful not to rototill it too finely or too frequently.

Jim ❖ When soil is pulverized—which can happen when you rototill too finely—its structure breaks down and becomes very dense, much like a loaf of bread made without yeast. The very fine soil particles end up fitting tightly together. When this happens, your soil becomes more vulnerable to wind and water erosion, and has very little air space for root growth. Properly structured soil has a blocky or columnar structure and is not densely packed.

Rototill a small area first, and then grab a fistful of soil to make sure it's not too fine. If your soil contains lots of organic matter, it is less likely to become pulverized or compacted.

Saving Seed

Can I save Non-Stop begonia tubers?

Lois ❖ Yes, but I don't recommend it.

Jim ❖ You'll have some serious obstacles to overcome.

• The tubers you harvest may have been produced by plants that have been started from seed and not be big enough to produce vigorous plants next year. Tubers form when the day length drops below 12 hours. In the northern hemisphere, this occurs around September 21—which roughly coincides with our first fall frost. Unless your climate is warmer than ours, your begonia tubers won't have time to develop fully.

• Tubers may become diseased during the growing season.

• Tubers are difficult to store. You need a consistently cool, dark, and moist spot.

• You must start tubers early—February is best—so you must start them in your home early to produce blooming plants in summer.

Do seeds keep indefinitely? How do I store my seeds?

Relative Storage Life of Seeds

Short
Anemone
Asparagus Fern
Aster
Begonia
Browallia
Delphinium
Impatiens
Pansy
Phlox
Salvia
Vinca
Viola

Medium
Ageratum
Alyssum
Celosia
Coleus
Cyclamen
Dahlia
Dianthus
Dusty Miller
Geranium
Lisianthus
Lobelia
Marigold
Petunia
Portulaca
Snapdragon
Verbena

Long
Amaranthus
Shasta Daisy
Stocks
Sweet Pea
Zinnia

Lois ❖ Seeds will not keep forever. Some seeds have a very short shelf-life—for example, pansies, impatiens, and many varieties of herbs—while others last a long time. I've had good results keeping my nasturium, sweet pea, and zinnia seeds. I always store my seeds in an old Tupperware container, though any airtight container will do just fine. Throw in a packet of dessicant, store it in a cool, dark room, and you're set!

Jim ❖ Typically, germination rates decrease a few percentage points for every year that a seed is stored. Those seeds that do germinate may produce less vigourous plants. A properly stored seed will not only germinate well when planted, but will also produce a robust and healthy plant.

You can take certain steps to maximize the storage life of your seeds. For example, every 1% decrease in moisture content and every 5°C decrease in storage temperature (down to the freezing mark) doubles the shelf-life (viability) of your seed. In other words, keep your seeds cool and dry. Never leave your seed packages open even for a short time—after only two hours, the seeds begin to draw humidity from the air. But don't simply fold the tops of the packs over. Put them in airtight containers with a silica gel desiccant, then store them in a cold room.

If I harvest seeds from this year's plants, will they grow as well as the seeds I buy in stores do?

Lois ❖ Because commercial seed companies carefully regulate and test their products, the seeds you buy in stores will germinate more reliably than those you collect from your plants. Also, seed harvesting and storage is a tricky process—if you don't do it right, you may be disappointed.

However, you'll only learn if you try. Collect your seeds only from non-hybrid plants, because otherwise the offspring won't resemble the parents. In the spring, start your harvested seeds a little bit earlier than normal, just in case they don't germinate. That way, you'll still have plenty of time to purchase seed.

Jim ❖ You run several risks when you harvest your own seeds. "Green seeds," seeds harvested before they're fully mature, won't germinate even if you dry them thoroughly. You might also encounter seed-borne diseases that can't be detected by the home gardener. If you fail to store your seeds properly, they may deteriorate rapidly.

Feel free to try harvesting your own seed, like Mom says, but I prefer to stick with professional seed companies. That way, I can be confident that I'm starting my garden off with the best and most dependable seed possible.

At Ball Seed Company, testing is done to determine germination and usable plant to arrive at a 'seed vigour' index.

What annuals are good for fall seeding?

Lois ❖ Any plants which readily self-seed, for example, cosmos, violas, or pansies.

Overwintering

Can I overwinter annuals as houseplants?

Lois ❖ Most annuals are not suitable for overwintering because light levels are too low in your house. However, if you have a very sunny, south-facing window or a sun room it's always worth a try.

Jim ❖ One word of caution if you decide to overwinter plants from your garden. Be careful to isolate the plants when you first bring them inside. Insect pests that are not a problem in the garden can cause problems indoors.

What varieties can I overwinter? How?

Lois ❖ Geraniums and fuchsia are probably two of your best choices.

Jim ❖ Keep the stock plant as cool as possible and the soil dry. No warmer than 14°C, but a few degrees cooler than that would be even better.

- Keep the plant in a bright area, but away from direct sunlight—direct sun can cause overheating.

- Early in the new year, move the plants from "storage" to a warmer, brighter area. A solarium would be ideal.

- In early February, harvest cuttings from the mother plants. Root the cuttings (see section on cuttings, earlier in this chapter), then discard the mother plants. Many of your cuttings will fail to root because your home doesn't offer the same ideal conditions as a greenhouse. It's still worth a try, however, if you're up to the challenge!

My mandevilla vine looks really scrawny. I overwintered it in the house and I think it did much better last year than this year. How do I overwinter a mandevilla vine properly?

Lois ❖ Mandevilla love lots of sunlight. The problem with growing them in the house over winter is the low light levels both inside and out. If you overwinter them in a sunny but cool room, they will look healthier come next spring.

Jim ❖ Mandevillas do best in their native subtropical climate. They prefer bright, direct sunlight and long days for vine and flower production. When you bring them inside for the winter, they have a difficult time adjusting to the lower light levels. They stop flowering and drop their leaves. If you can, give them more light, this problem won't be as bad. Find a room, preferably cool, with a bright, south-facing window, and you'll have a much healthier mandevilla. In the spring, cut it back and fertilize to promote healthy new growth.

Interestingly, although they're adapted to warmer regions, mandevillas can take a surprising amount of frost, although not for extended periods. A mandevilla of mine once survived -3 °C temperatures without a problem.

I've noticed petunias are propagated from cuttings. Why? Can I overwinter mine and start my own?

Lois ❖ I wouldn't recommend it. Petunias are very difficult to overwinter in the house. Low winter light levels, dry air, and warm temperatures provide a poor growing environment for petunias.

Jim ❖ This question applies to overwintering plants in general. Let's compare overwintering plants at home versus greenhouses.

- **Light Levels:** Light provides energy for plant growth. Light levels in greenhouses are often 30 times higher than those in your home. Your house can provide enough light to overwinter plants such as geraniums and fuchsias, but not enough to grow vigorous cuttings.

- **Temperature:** Most temperate zone plants do best when the temperature remains at a consistent level between 16 and 18°C. That's all right for a greenhouse, but unless you have a good collection of sweaters, this is probably cooler than you'd like to keep your house. At normal room temperatures and low light, plants use up their food reserves more quickly.

- **Humidity:** The humidity levels can be optimized in a greenhouse. While some houses do have this control, the air in most houses is positively arid in the winter.

- **Pests:** Most greenhouses maintain very strict standards and can test and treat disease. At home, pests are tough to control. The average home gardener also isn't trained or equipped to identify pests and diseases. Many plants harbour diseases that can only be diagnosed with special test equipment.

End of Season

I want to save seeds from my non-hybrid annuals. How do I collect the seeds?

Lois ❖ Saving seed is actually a simple process. Ensure the seeds have fully matured on your plant. Cut a stem off of your plant, turn it upside down over a bucket, and knock it against the sides to shake out the seed. Dry the seed then store in a cool, dark location in an airtight container.

Jim ❖ Mom's right, saving seed is easy, but timing is the key. If you collect seed too early it will be "green" or immature. If you wait too long, the seed heads shatter, scattering the seeds before you have a chance to collect them. Harvest your seed heads as soon as they become brown and dry.

How should I prepare my flowerbeds in the fall for the next growing season?

Lois ❖ Though it's tempting to let the garden slip into disarray, a little work in the fall goes a long way towards ensuring a great garden next year. The most important fall job is to clean up the garden. That means removing dead foliage and removing any weeds that may still be growing in your flowerbeds.

Jim ❖ Some people prefer to leave their garden clean-up until the following spring. The dead plants do help to anchor the snow cover, and they don't cause any real harm provided that they are free of disease.

However, dead foliage can harbour pests and disease, and looks dreadful over the course of the winter. I prefer to roll up my sleeves and get the job over with in the fall, weather permitting.

Should I just turn my dead plants under in the fall?

Lois ❖ Yes, if you can—a rototiller is great for these chores. You can do this for some of your plants, but those with thick or woody stalks might take several years to fully decompose. Any diseased plants should be disposed of to prevent the disease from spreading.

Jim ❖ We always work everything into the ground because we have a big rototiller. However, in small beds we remove plants and add compost or peat moss every year to keep the levels of organic material high.

Salpiglossis 'Royale Pale Blue Bicolour'

CHAPTER 5
TROUBLESHOOTING

Gardening is a complex endeavor, and plenty of problems, large and small, can crop up in the course of each season. Early in the bedding-plant business, we lost a whole crop of marigolds because we'd left our store of 2,4-D weed killer in a loft that was far too close to the plants. We were a little embarrassed when we figured out what had happened, but we learned how powerful such chemicals really are; it was a valuable eye-opener. It's not easy to do, but try to take your setbacks with a sense of humour. They're part of the experience, after all, and there's a certain sense of morbid fun in comparing garden horror stories.

Problems with Soil

Is it possible to over-fertilize?
How can I tell if I've done it?

Lois ❖ If your plants have been over-fertilized, they will look as if they've been singed, with dry, brown edges.

Jim ❖ When you over-fertilize, water ends up flowing out of the roots instead of into them. The plant begins to dry up, and the edges of the leaves turn brown. That's what people mean when they say that fertilizer "burns" plants.

Your plants can also suffer if they're given unbalanced fertilizer. For example, too much nitrogen (the first of the three numbers on a fertilizer label) causes excessive top growth, especially on such plants as petunias and nicotiana. Avoid adding too much rich compost, which is high in nitrogen.

My pansies look deformed. The flowers are misshapen, and the stems are thick and flat. My lawn was recently sprayed for weeds. Could the chemicals have harmed my pansies?

Lois ❖ This can easily happen. One year, I remember, we were growing flats of seedlings in the greenhouses adjacent to our garage. We had stored some 2,4-D weed killer inside the garage, and the breeze blowing through the garage was enough to expose our seedlings to a harmful amount of the fumes.

Jim ❖ 2,4-D can seriously distort your plants, particularly the new growth. People often forget how careful you have to be when applying any kind of herbicide. This sounds like the probable culprit in your case, and I'm afraid it's untreatable.

The other possible culprit is a boron deficiency in your soil, which can cause thick, flat leaves. If a soil test confirms that this is your problem, add B+ iron sulphate to the soil.

Sunflower 'Ikarus'

Weather

Some of the leaves on my bedding plants are white along the edges. What could cause this?

Lois ❖ My friend's little grandson once saw this in his backyard and wondered why it had snowed on the edges of the flowers! The white markings are usually caused by low temperatures. Don't worry, it's nothing serious. Your plants will be fine once the temperatures warm up.

Jim ❖ The white edges are destroyed plant tissue. The cold temperatures damage the leaf cells along the edges. Most of the damage occurs on the newest growth. As Mom says, it's only a temporary setback.

Why are the leaves on my plants turning red/purple?

Lois ❖ Low temperatures can quickly turn geranium leaves red and marigold leaves purple. Just like the white edging on your leaves, this is only a minor, temporary problem.

Jim ❖ The redness on your leaves could also be caused by a nutrient deficiency, usually phosphorus or nitrogen. If the problem persists, you should get your soil tested (see Chapter 1).

However, if the weather has been cool, or if you only recently transplanted your plants, Mom's explanation is most likely the case.

Salvia 'Strata'

My flowerbed was ravaged by hail. Will the plants recover?

Lois ❖ Most flowerbeds will recover completely, even after a severe hailstorm, provided that it happens early enough in the season. A few years ago, a May hailstorm took everyone in St. Albert completely by surprise. I was sure all my flowers were ruined, but in a week or two they were just fine. Patience is the key! Your beds will look just awful right after the storm, but they'll usually recover. I like to give my plants an extra boost of fertilizer after a hail storm to help them recover more quickly.

A late-summer hailstorm can be a different story. Mature plants, once damaged by hail, will never be quite the same. If you're lucky, though, they'll recover partially.

It snowed last night and I was unable to cover my annual plants. Will they be okay?

Lois ❖ You might end up being very thankful for that snow! It's a very good insulator. Provided the temperature didn't dip too far below freezing, the blanket of snow was likely enough to completely protect your plants from damage. If it continues to be cold overnight for the next few days, put a cover over the plants and let the snow protect them.

Jim ❖ Most annuals are pretty resilient, particularly early in the growing season. I bet your plants will bounce back better than ever, thanks to all the moisture from the melting snow.

Pests and Problems
Pests

Some of my annuals have a silver film on the leaves. What could cause this?

Lois ❖ This silver film is caused by slugs. They leave a silvery trail of mucous as they travel across your flowers. There are all kinds of ways to get rid of slugs in your gardens, but I've always simply just trapped them or removed them as I see them because slugs generally aren't a problem here. One way to help prevent slug problems is to ensure your garden is free of debris (the places where slugs like to hide).

Jim ❖ Slugs are not a huge problem in Alberta; however, in many areas of the country they can be. There are several methods available to control slugs. Safer's Slug and Snail Bait controls slugs organically. You can also use any slug bait that has metaldehyde as an active ingredient .

The flower buds on my geraniums open slowly and when they finally flower, they seem distorted and marked. What's wrong?

Jim ❖ This is likely due to small insects called thrips. Thrips are very tiny, needle-like insects that love the pollen in flowers. When they feed, they distort the flowers and can also cause the buds to turn brown. The best way to check for thrips is to do the "tap test." Break off a petiole (flower) from your geranium and tap it sharply several times on a white sheet of paper. If any thrips fall out, you'll easily spot them against the paper.

Lisianthus 'Florida Sky Blue'

The new growth on my mandevilla is covered in small green bugs. What are they?

Lois ❖ They are aphids, also known as green fly. Although they are very prolific, they're easy to control if caught early.

Jim ❖ Although aphids are rather easy to kill, they remain one of the worst insect pests in gardens. The reason is simple—they reproduce at an astounding rate. During the spring and summer, aphids produce live young rather than eggs, and females do not require a male for the production of offspring.

Control of aphids depends on viligance. Check mandevilla each day—aphids prefer new growth so inspect the shoots thoroughly. Insecticidal soap will control aphids provided it is applied early enough.

Aphids

Pesticides

Instead of using insecticidal soap, can I treat bedding plants with my own dish-soap solution? If so, how much should I dilute it?

Lois ❖ You can use regular soap, but never use detergent! It contains harsh cleansers that will dissolve leaf waxes and burn your plants.

Jim ❖ Insecticidal soap is more refined than regular types of soap. It's also relatively inexpensive. Hand soaps often contain compounds that can burn plants. However, if you're not too worried about the risk, you can try using hand soap by making a 1% solution (10 ml of soap in 1 litre of water). If you find that your brand of hand soap works well and doesn't injure your plants, you can continue to use it.

Whether you use insecticidal or regular soap, spray or soak the foliage thoroughly. The soap has to actually contact the pest. Soaps have very little effect on hard-shelled insects such as beetles, but they work well on small, soft-bodied pests like aphids.

Diseases

What is that white film on the leaves of my begonias? I think it's killing them.

Lois ❖ That white stuff is a fungal disease called powdery mildew. It looks like talcum powder sprinkled across the leaves. Treat it right away—it spreads quickly.

Jim ❖ There are many different species of powdery mildew; the kind that attacks your begonias differs from the kind that attacks your roses. Whatever the species, though, powdery mildew is a nasty, persistent threat to your plants.

How does powdery mildew spread?

Jim ❖ The mildew typically begins as a very tiny spore that lands on your leaf. It remains dormant until it gets the moisture it needs for germination. Once the leaf gets moist and stays moist for about three hours (say, from overhead sprinkling or condensation on a cool, moist night), the mildew begins to develop. It rapidly spreads in white strands (hyphae) across the face of the leaf, dropping pegs (haustoria) into the leaf to anchor it and allow it to draw nutrients from your plant. At that point, it doesn't need any more leaf-surface moisture to proliferate—it can get all it needs directly from within the leaves.

Powdery mildew tends to attack plants that are already vulnerable for one reason or another. Anything that weakens the plant allows the mildew to penetrate the leaf surface more easily. For instance, plants that don't get enough sunlight tend to have thinner leaves, making them more prone to infection. Plants deficient in nutrients (calcium in particular) have weaker leaf-cell walls and are also more vulnerable.

How do I treat powdery mildew?

Jim ❖ Once powdery mildew takes hold, it is very difficult to control—in fact, I have yet to find an effective spray to halt the disease's progress. Your best bet is preventative control. Spray susceptible plants (begonias, roses) before you even see the first sign of mildew. Spray every seven to ten days using benomyl. Some people also like to use baking soda: about a 15 mL per 4L of water (1 tablespoon per gallon) combined with a 10% solution of summer plant oil. Always experiment on a few leaves before treating the whole plant to ensure the spray does no damage.

Snapdragon 'Ribbon Crimson'

Problems

Someone told me that people who smoke or handle tobacco can infect their plants with a disease. Which plants can be infected, and what is the disease?

Lois ❖ The disease they're referring to, *Tobacco Mosaic Virus*, can be spread from tobacco to the plants. If you do smoke, wash your hands before gardening.

Jim ❖ The tobacco plant comes from the Solanaceae family, which includes tomato, nicotiana, petunia, and calibrachoa. These plants are all at risk for Tomato Mosaic Virus (ToMV) and Tobacco Mosaic Virus (TMV), two highly infectious diseases. Leaf debris from an infected plant can remain infectious for up to two years in dry soil.

The disease gets its name from yellow spots that cover the leaves in a mosaic-like pattern. Once TMV hits, there's little you can do to fight it, apart from carefully removing and destroying any infected foliage. The best cure is prevention. Like Mom says, be sure to wash your hands after handling or smoking tobacco.

Sweet Potato Vine

Venidium 'Jaffa Ice'

My plants are turning yellow and going limp. What could be causing this?

Lois ❖ It sounds as if your soil is waterlogged. Be careful not to overwater your beds. Next year, before planting, work plenty of sand into your soil to improve the drainage.

Jim ❖ You can tell if drainage is the problem by grabbing and squeezing a handful of your moist soil. If it compacts into a muddy, clay-like ball, your soil has inadequate drainage. Properly drained soil allows excess water to pass through, leaving tiny air spaces. If this doesn't happen, the roots become waterlogged. They can't absorb any oxygen and begin to die. Above ground, this translates into yellow, wilted foliage.

If you're growing your plants in containers, check to make sure that they all have drainage holes.

I water every day, but my plants are still wilting. What's wrong?

Lois ❖ You may be watering every day, but if you don't water properly, the plants will not receive enough moisture. A little daily sprinkling doesn't penetrate beyond the top layer of soil. Your plants greatly prefer a deep, thorough soaking every few days. Plants in hanging baskets or containers, may require daily watering, however.

Jim ❖ Many factors can cause wilting, but here's a lineup of the usual suspects:

- The plants aren't being watered thoroughly enough.

- The plants are newly transplanted and the roots haven't grown into the soil. The moisture in the root ball is being pulled away by the dryer surrounding soil.

- Root rot has taken hold, and the diseased roots can no longer supply the leaves with enough moisture on warm days. If your soil is *too* moist, this may be the problem.

- The soil is too salty, causing the plant roots to lose water instead of drawing it in.

- The soil is cold compared to the warm leaves. The constricted roots can't draw up water until the soil warms up. Fuchsias are especially prone to this. If you water your plants with icy-cold water, try switching to luke-warm instead.

Flowering Kale 'Dynasty Pink'

CHAPTER 6 🦋
VARIETIES

What's good for the gazania isn't necessarily good for the godetia. Different plant species have different needs, a fact that's reinforced every year when Valerie conducts in-the-field tests, called trials, on hundreds of different bedding-plant varieties. These trials have revealed all kinds of valuable information about growth habits. Last year, Valerie put the new Tidal Wave petunias through their paces. She planted one group with a 30-cm space between each plant, and another group with 90-cm spacing. The petunias that were planted more densely responded by forming a tall tsunami of colour—a true tidal wave. The less closely packed plants, with more room to spread out, grew into shorter, more widespread waves. Both groups looked absolutely gorgeous, but it's handy to know that you have some control over the ultimate form these plants take.

Wе have collected many questions that are specific to varieties. Here they are, arranged in alphabetical order, with the answers.

Ageratum

Why are my ageratum flowers turning brown and mushy?

Lois ❖ This is usually caused by overhead watering. The flowers of ageratum are thick clusters of fine petals that tend to catch and hold the water. Rot can then set in the centre of the flowers. Try directing the watering spray towards the soil, avoiding the flowers. This should alleviate the problem.

Alyssum/Bacopa

My alyssum/bacopa leaves are full of tiny holes. What could be the cause?

Jim ❖ Alyssum is related to the cole crops (cabbage, cauliflower, and broccoli), which are all susceptible to flea beetle. These tiny black beetles (some with orange stripes) chew small holes into the leaves. Spray with an insecticide containing permethrin. Diazinon, while effective on many insects, doesn't work as well on flea beetles.

Ageratum 'Hawaii Blue'

Amaranthus

I have several amaranthus of the "Love Lies Bleeding" variety. All the plants have produced nice long ropes, but they are green. When will they turn red?

Jim ❖ They will never turn red; the colour of the "ropes" is not a factor of maturity. Love lies bleeding tends to be the common name for all "rope-type" amaranthus. It is the species *Amaranthus caudathus* that produces long crimson ropes. *Amaranthus viridis,* or "green tails," is likely the species you have—its ropes are green.

Asters

Every year I plant asters but they never bloom until the end of the summer. Is there anything I can do to make them bloom earlier in the season?

Lois ❖ Asters naturally bloom later in the growing season. You'll either have to start your seeds much earlier or buy larger, more mature bedding plants.

Jim ❖ Your problem has to do with day length. Asters are long-day plants, which means that they require lots of daylight—14 to 16-hour days over the course of several weeks—before they produce flowers. Everywhere on earth, the days and nights are of equal length (give or take a few minutes) around March 21. Here in the northern hemisphere, day length increases from that date, reaching the maximum length on June 21. So sometime in late April the days will be long enough to trigger flowering.

You can force your asters to flower earlier by artificially increasing day length through the use of grow lights.

Begonias

What is the difference between fibrous and tuberous begonias?

Lois ❖ Fibrous begonias (also called wax begonias) are short, compact plants with small, single flowers. They are excellent for border plants in shady areas. Tuberous begonias, on the other hand, are big and bushy, with large, showy, mostly double flowers. They are very colourful and are one of our most popular hanging baskets.

Jim ❖ Fibrous and tuberous begonias are actually two different species, *Begonia* x *semperflorens* and *Begonia* x *tuberhybrida*. New trailing begonias like the Dragon Wing are a hybrid of fibrous begonias and are identified as *B.* x *hybrida*.

What is the difference between Non-Stop tuberous begonias and traditional tuberous begonias?

Lois ❖ Non-Stop begonias really live up to their name! Compared with traditional begonias, the individual flowers are a bit smaller—but each plant is very prolific. Non-Stop begonias have a mounding growth habit, and the flowers are produced on the top of the plants, making them extremely showy. Traditional tuberous begonias produce fewer flowers, but the flowers are larger and available in many different colours and bicolour combinations. The plants have a much more upright growth habit, and the flowers are produced close to the main stem.

Jim ❖ Because Non-Stop begonias are seed-bred, they are also cheaper than traditional begonias. Traditional begonias still have their loyal fans, however, because they can produce such large, spectactular blooms.

Can begonia plants be split?

Lois ❖ No. Both fibrous and tuberous plants would be damaged. Always start your begonias from seed, tubers, or new plants.

Jim ❖ You can take cuttings from your begonias, but because these stems are very fleshy, even this procedure can be challenging.

Can I save the tubers of Non-Stop begonias?

Lois ❖ I never save Non-Stop tubers. They seldom produce tubers large enough to overwinter successfully, so I don't recommend them for storage.

My begonia plants always rot.
What am I doing wrong?

Lois ❖ You may have started off with soft tubers to begin with. Check your tubers for soft spots and injuries.

Jim ❖ Rot can generally be caused by any combination of the following conditions:

- Poor air circulation.
- Overhead watering (water remains on the leaves and stems).
- Poor drainage (wet soil).
- Crowded conditions (weaker growth is more susceptible to disease).
- Watering in the evening when nights are cool.

Can I plant my begonias in full sun
and then water them more often?

Lois ❖ Fibrous and tuberous begonias both prefer some shade, along with warm, moist soil. They won't perform well in full sun, no matter how well they are watered.

Jim ❖ Remember, however, that most begonias will grow well in partially sunny locations or filtered sunlight with a little extra water.

Begonia 'Dragon Wing'

Why does my tuberous begonia plant have both double and single flowers on it? Is something wrong with it?

Lois ❖ Your begonia plant is fine. Tuberous begonias often bear two types of flowers: the showy double flowers (female) and a lesser number of single blooms (male).

Jim ❖ That's true for begonias, but not necessarily for other plants in your garden. Flowering plants fall into different categories such as:

- Monoecious: Individual plants produce both male and female flowers (begonias are monoecious).
- Dioecious: Each individual plant produces only male flowers, or only female flowers.
- Perfect flowers: Every flower contains both the male (stamen) and female (stigma) organs. "Imperfect flowers," such as those on monoecious and dioecious plants, carry only male or only female sexual organs.

As for begonias, remember that pinching off the single flowers results in larger double blooms.

Bells of Ireland

Do bells of Ireland plants produce flowers?

Lois ❖ If you're thinking of traditional-looking flowers, no, but the blooms this plant produces are both beautiful and unusual. The flowers are long stems covered with bright-green, bell-shaped blooms, 5 cm long. They make wonderful cutflowers.

Browallia

My browallia looks healthy but it is the same size it was when I planted it. What's wrong?

Lois ❖ Browallia likes some shade, but it also prefers warm temperatures. Chances are your plant is just waiting patiently for warmer weather!

Jim ❖ Browallia won't grow when temperatures are in the low teens. As long as your plant looks healthy, I don't think there's any cause for worry. You'll see a big difference once the days warm up.

Browallia 'Blue Bells'

Brugmansia & Datura

What is angel's trumpet? Is it easy to grow?

Lois ❖ Angel's trumpet is the common name for a large, spectacular plant called brugmansia. The plant itself is tall, reaching about 1 to 1.5 m, but it's the incredible flowers that everyone loves. Different varieties produce extra-large double or single bell-shaped blooms, in white, yellow, lilac, or salmon. My absolute favourite is salmon. And, yes, it's reasonably easy to grow.

Jim ❖ Angel's trumpet (also known as datura, thorn apple, or brugmansia) is a member of the solanaceae family, which also includes the potato, tomato, and petunia. Although tropical in origin, it grows well as an annual all across Canada. It likes lots of room, a warm sunny location, and regular fertilizer and water.

Technically, the term *datura* refers to the family of smaller plants with upright flowers, while those taller plants with large dangling flowers are called *brugmansia*. Collectively, though, these show-stopping plant are commonly called datura.

I want to grow my datura in a pot. What size of pot should I use?

Lois ❖ It always amazes me how vigorously datura grows. Over the years, I've seen many of mine grow big and bushy, up to 1.5 m tall. I prefer to use at least a 15-litre pot (or the largest container I can find)—otherwise, the plant becomes rootbound and practically impossible to keep watered and fed. Be creative—a friend of mine swore her datura grew best in a great big wash tub she plunked in a sunny corner of her yard.

Jim ❖ Datura/brugmansia in a pot will stop growing when it becomes rootbound. If you want it to keep growing, you must transplant it to a larger container. We pot up our datura several times each season as they get bigger. The fully grown specimens you may have seen in our greenhouse are in a 68-litre (15-gallon) pot.

The lower leaves on my datura are yellow. Now the upper leaves are beginning to turn yellow, too! What's wrong?

Lois ❖ Chances are, your datura is low on fertilizer. Step up your fertilizing rate, using just a pinch of 20-20-20 at every watering (see section on fertilizing).

Datura is also susceptible to spider mites, which often first manifests itself with yellowing of leaves, before you notice the insects.

Jim ❖ Mom's right. The problem is probably a lack of fertilizer. Datura are very heavy feeders. When any plant exhibits yellow lower leaves, it usually points to a deficiency of nitrogen (the first number on the label). The reason it shows up first on the lower leaves is that nitrogen is very mobile within a plant. When a plant is short on nitrogen, it robs it from the older leaves and shifts it to the areas that are actively growing. As a result, the leaves nearest the top are the last to turn yellow and pale.

If you suspect spidermites, check the undersides of the leaves for webbing and tiny, spider-like insects. Chemical controls for spider mites are available at most garden centres.

Fuchsia

What is the difference between trailing and upright fuchsias? Which one is hardier?

Lois ❖ As the names imply, trailing fuchsias are the ones you see overflowing the sides of hanging baskets, while upright fuchsias are bred to be taller and bushier. Both trailing and upright fuchsias are gorgeous, while neither can be considered hardy. If you want to keep enjoying them into the fall, you must cover them or bring them indoors when there's a threat of frost.

Jim ❖ Growers are currently doing a lot of breeding work on developing hardier upright varieties of this plant. These varieties are hardy to zone 7, dying back to the ground and then sprouting again the following spring, but that's not much help for most Canadians! In most parts of the country, these newer varieties will bloom from summer until the first hard frost, so they are best treated as annuals. Fortunately, the plants can be overwintered indoors, using the same methods as with geraniums.

My fuchsia is turning yellow and dropping all of its flowers and buds. What is wrong?

Lois ❖ These are the classic symptoms of a plant that isn't getting enough sunlight. Fuchsias don't do well in full sun or deep shade; they prefer a partially shady or partially sunny location.

What are those cherry-shaped things growing on my fuchsia? Should I pinch them off?

Lois ❖ Those are the seed pods. As with most flowering plants, it's a good idea to pinch off the dead blossoms before the seeds form. Deadheading fuchsias will encourage them to keep blooming, because all the plant's energy will go to the production of flowers instead of seeds.

Jim ❖ If you plan to overwinter your fuchsia, stop deadheading near the end of summer and allow the seed pods to form and ripen.

Can I save those seeds?

Jim ❖ It's possible (but not easy) to grow fuchsia from saved seeds. However, chances are the resulting plants won't be true to type, because most fuchsia are hybrids. It's best to take cuttings if you want to propagate your fuchsia.

Gazania

My gazania flowers always seem to be closed. Why?

Lois ❖ Gazania flowers close up on overcast days and at night. They'll open again when the sun returns.

Jim ❖ This is a characteristic that breeders are attempting to eliminate. In fact, my favourite gazania, the Daybreak series, produces large, brightly coloured flowers that will stay more fully open under cloudy conditions than older varieties.

Geraniums

What is the difference between zonal, hybrid, ivy, and vegetative geraniums?

Lois ❖ Vegetative geraniums refer to how the plants are propogated. Both zonal and ivy geraniums are produced from cuttings—or vegatatively propogated. Hybrid geraniums are produced from seed.

Jim ❖ Zonal geraniums (*Pelargonium* x *hortorum*), also commonly known as "double-flowered" geraniums, are the most common type of geranium. They are taller, upright plants with large double flowerheads produced on long stems. They grow well in almost any garden setting. Designer geraniums are my favourite zonal types because of their excellent growth habit and vibrant colours.

Ivy geraniums (*Pelargonium peltatum*), or "hanging" geraniums, have a trailing growth habit and smooth, waxy leaves. The flowers are usually medium-sized with double flowers and semi-double florets. They grow best in hanging baskets, window boxes, and patio planters.

Hybrid geraniums (*Pelargonium* x *hortorum* 'hybrid') are seed produced and also have an upright growth habit, but they are shorter and bushier than zonal geraniums. They produce many medium to smaller-sized, single-petalled flowerheads. They are ideal for window boxes and an excellent choice for border or mass plantings in flowerbeds.

Gazania 'Daybreak Orange'

What is an ivy/zonal geranium?

Lois ❖ It is a plant bred to have characteristics of both ivy and zonal geraniums. I rocommend the Galleria series for those who want ivy/zonal geraniums.

Jim ❖ This is a fairly recent breeding development. Ivy/zonal geraniums are great-looking plants that combine the cascading habit of an ivy geranium with the large, round flowerheads of zonal geraniums. They are vegetatively propogated and their leaves resemble those of zonal geraniums.

What is a European ivy geranium?

Lois ❖ These are a type of ivy geraniums commonly found throughout Europe, hence the name. European ivy geraniums have smaller, waxy leaves and masses of single flowers which cover the plants' vigourous, arching branches. If you have ever seen a postcard of a summer chalet in the Swiss Alps, these are the gorgeous red and pink flowers tumbling from the chalet window boxes.

Jim ❖ Recent breeding developments have brought these plants back to the forefront. They lost popularity in North America in the '70s because of their leggy growth habit and limited blooms. New varieties have a mounding, vigorous growth habit and are coverd in flowers.

What is the difference between Martha Washington geraniums and pansy geraniums?

Lois ❖ These are actually two common names for *Pelargonium* x *domesticum*, also known as regal geraniums. Regal geraniums have spectacular large, open-faced flowers with dark blotches (somewhat like pansies, hence the common name) and fragrant serrated leaves. They come in gorgeous colour combinations from deep salmon to mauve and make great accent plants.

Do you have any special tips for deadheading geraniums?

Lois ❖ Your plants look much cleaner if you remove as much of the stem as possible when you deadhead. My main tip, though, is to just snap off the stems rather than cutting them with scissors. This is easier if you deadhead before the flowerheads get too old and do your deadheading early in the day.

Jim ❖ When the petioles (the stems that support the flower) are cool, they snap off more easily. That's why Mom says it's easier to do it in the morning. Later in the day, when the petioles become softer, you're better off using scissors.

Do geraniums tolerate frost?

Lois ❖ Yes. From my experience, toughened, acclimatized geraniums are good to about - 4°C for several hours. They can survive colder temperatures, but suffer considerable damage.

Geranium 'Designer Picotee Salmon'

I saw a geranium that was huge, as big as a bush! Is this a special variety?

Lois ❖ Most likely, what you saw was an old plant that had been overwintered and then replanted in the spring—you can tell by the woody-looking stem. In mild regions, the zonal geranium is a perennial.

The buds on my geranium are turning brown and drying up before they open. What's the problem?

Lois ❖ This question is really impossible to answer without seeing your plant. However, the most common cause tends to be low light.

Jim ❖ Flower production requires higher light levels than leaf production. People often purchase a flowering geranium plant and put it in their house or garage. Eventually low light levels cause the buds to dry up while the plant itself seems healthy. Not to worry, your geranium will begin to bloom again when it is planted outside in your garden.

Godetia

My godetia is getting long and leggy. What should I do to make it look full again?

Lois ❖ Godetia can get messy looking and should be pinched early and often to encourage branching. Remove the flowers as soon as they're spent. I've also discovered that they do best in cool soil, out of the way of the afternoon sun.

My mother used to grow godetia in her garden years ago, and the variety she grew had very small flowers. Why?

Lois ❖ The variety your mother grew was probably an older species type. Breeding and hybridization over the years have produced varieties with larger, showier flowers. There are also many different species of godetia, and flower size varies from species to species. For example, *Godetia bottae*, *Godetia grandiflora*, and *Godetia whitney* tend to produce larger (5 cm) flowers, while *Godetia rublicunda* produces smaller (3 cm) flowers.

Jim ❖ Your mother may have been growing a single-flowering clarkia species in her garden, which is in the same family (Onagraceae) as godetia. Clarkia can look very similar to godetia.

Ice Plant & Portulaca

Are ice plant and Livingstone daisies the same plant?

Lois ❖ No. Two separate species are commonly referred to as "ice plant" because of their remarkably similar flowers. To avoid confusion, we call *Delosperma* spp. "ice plant from cuttings" and *Mesembryanthemum crystallinum* "Livingstone daisy."

Jim ❖ The important difference between these plants is the way in which they are propagated. Livingstone daisy can be grown from seed by home gardeners, while ice plants are generally vegetatively propogated.

What are the differences between the different kinds of portulaca?

Lois ❖ Two different species of plants go by the common name portulaca. *Portulaca grandiflora*, which we at the greenhouse call "portulaca," is a low-growing species with medium-size, rose-like double blooms. *Portulaca oleracea*, which we call "portulaca from cuttings," is a trailing plant with small, single-petalled, open flowers. Both make excellent annual groundcovers. Portulaca from cuttings also grows well in a container or hanging basket. Both species love full sun and heat and are fairly drought tolerant.

Jim ❖ Once again, the important difference for home gardeners lies in how these plants are propagated. *Portulaca grandiflora* can be sown indoors 8 to 10 weeks before transplanting into the garden, while *Portulaca oleracea* should be purchased as bedding plants.

Why do the flowers on my portulaca and ice plant close when it's cloudy?

Lois ❖ They're saving their pollen for a sunny day! It is interesting to note that a lot of breeding work is being done to develop new varieties whose flowers remain open, even on cloudy days.

Jim ❖ Pollinating insects don't like to go out when it's cool and wet. By closing shop during bad weather, portulacas and ice plants protect their pollen from the wind and rain. Then, once the sun comes out, they open their doors for business once again.

CHAPTER 6 ❧ VARIETIES

Portulaca and ice plant are drought tolerant. Should I still water them?

Lois ❖ You should definitely water the plants regularly until they are established. After that, water only when the plants are dry. Neither of these plants likes being consistently wet.

Impatiens

My friend has an impatiens plant that reseeds itself. What is it?

Lois ❖ If it is quite tall—about 1.5 m—it is likely a Himalayan impatiens. These plants readily reseed themselves. They're wonderful plants, despite their tendency to get a bit weedy-looking. They grow tall and large, with reddish stems and leaves, and gorgeous pink flowers.

Jim ❖ Himalayan impatiens reseeds itself readily and can become quite invasive if left untended. Be prepared to control it if you don't want it to take over your flowerbed.

How much shade can impatiens take?

Lois ❖ Impatiens grow in shadier areas, but they do not grow well in deep shade, especially in areas with cooler summers.

Jim ❖ Impatiens will do just fine as long as they receive bright indirect sunlight—partial shade to partial sun.

Can I plant impatiens in a sunny location?

Lois ❖ Yes, but impatiens may not grow well if the location is too hot and dry. They'll probably be fine for most of the summer, but watch out if the temperature climbs into the high 20s or low 30s!

Jim ❖ This really varies from region to region. Impatiens can tolerate full sun in cool coastal regions, but doesn't do well in the blazing heat of the prairie summer. Remember to keep them well watered, particularly on warm days.

Q&A ❧ BEDDING PLANTS *117*

What is a double-flowering impatiens?

Lois ❖ Double-flowering impatiens are impatiens with fully double, rose-like flowers. They have a bushy, mounding growth habit and are great for hanging baskets. They are not as tolerant of shade as regular impatiens but do not like full sun. My favourites are the Fiesta series: they are smothered in 100% fully double, vividly coloured flowers and have a wonderfully bushy, vigourous growth habit.

Can I grow double-flowering impatiens from seed?

Lois ❖ Yes; however the best varieties (like the Fiesta series) are still vegetatively propagated. If you do want to try growing double impatiens from seed, try 'Carousel.' It is the best double-flowering impatiens from seed to date.

Jim ❖ If you want to try seeding some, start the seeds indoors 6 to 8 weeks before the average last frost date, and transplant them 8 to 10 weeks later, once the soil has had a chance to warm up a bit.

I planted New Guinea impatiens in the shade—it didn't grow well. Why?

Lois ❖ Unlike standard impatiens, New Guinea impatiens actually prefers a sunny location, although it will tolerate some light shade. In southerly areas like Texas and Florida, it should be planted in a location that protects it from the hot afternoon sun, but for most gardeners a location with lots of sun is the best choice. The trick to growing New Guinea impatiens successfully is sun, warmth, regular water, and well-drained soil. My personal favourites are the Celebration series, with more than 20 flower and foliage colours.

Jim ❖ New Guinea impatiens has really increased in popularity over the past few years. The earlier varieties required lots of heat to perform well in the garden, and our cooler summers just were not conducive to growing these plants successfully. We actually dropped them for a while because of their poor performance in the garden. However, recent breeding advances have transformed these plants into one of our most popular annuals.

Kochia

Why does kochia turn red more in some years than others?

Lois ❖ Sometimes, if the late summer and fall are especially cool and wet, the kochia plants don't turn colour before a killing frost. It is also interesting to note that some of the newer varieties of kochia remain green; their leaves never turn red in fall.

Jim ❖ Chlorophyll is the green pigment in plants. It is also the primary light-gathering compound in the leaves. However, other pigments, such as xanthophyll and anthocyanin, also harvest light.

For most of the season, anthocyanin, a red pigment, is masked by the green chlorophyll. In the fall, though, the chlorophyll gradually breaks down, revealing the anthocyanin. This is why trees rich in anthocyanin (such as maples) turn a vibrant red in the fall.

Like maples, kochia plants produce plenty of anthocyanin. If the late summer days are particularly warm and the nights are particularly cool, your kochia will producer higher levels of anthocyanin. That's why they turn red more in some years.

Lavatera

I have a hard time growing lavatera. Can you give me some tips?

Lavatera 'Silver Cup'

Lois ❖ Although lavatera grows vigorously in the garden, it can be tricky to germinate and transplant. Its roots don't tolerate disturbance well, making transplanting a challenge. If you are starting lavatera seed indoors, plant the seed directly into the pot in which the plant will grow until it is transplanted into the garden. Lavatera requires lots of direct sunlight and doesn't like its roots to dry out or stay too wet. Although I don't often recommend fungicides, be prepared to use a preventive such as No Damp when you seed lavatera. I have also talked to many people who have had better success seeding lavatera directly into their garden, instead of starting it from seed indoors.

Jim ❖ In general, lavatera is susceptible to disease. Some of these disease organisms are present in the soil (so always use a clean soilless potting mixture) and some of them are present in the seed coat. Some of the wholesale companies are now selling seed that has been stripped of its outer layer—and thus, its first site of infection. The seeds are then coated with a film that protects them against soil-borne disease during emergence and increases their resistance to disease.

Lisianthus

Why does my lisianthus wilt even when it is well watered?

Jim ❖ Lisianthus (*Eustoma grandiflora*) is susceptible to several different soil diseases. At the visible bud stage, it can develop root rot or crown rot. (The crown of the plant is the junction where the roots change to stem. Any disease that attacks the root or crown is considered a root or crown rot disease.) Once infected, the plant tends to wilt during the day and recover somewhat overnight. Over the course of a week or ten days, it gradually succumbs to the disease. To prevent root and crown rot, keep lisianthus moist but never overly wet and plant it in well-drained soil in a warm, sunny location.

Lobelia

What's the difference between bush and trailing lobelia?

Lois ❖ Bush and trailing lobelia are different varieties of the same species. The main difference lies in their growth habits. Bush lobelia tends to form small, 10-cm-tall mounds, while trailing lobelia induces 30-cm-long stems of pendent (dangling) flowers.

My lobelia is choking out most of the flowers in my hanging basket. How can I prevent this?

Lois ❖ It's always a good idea to combine plants with similar growth habits. Lobelia is a vigourous grower, so combine it with other vigorously growing annuals. Alternatively, use more mature bedding plants, ones that are large compared to your younger lobelia. That way, they'll have a jump-start in size prior to planting up your basket.

Jim ❖ Plants such as ivy geraniums will be better able to keep up with lobelia's fast growth rate.

Can lobelia grow in full sun?

Lois ❖ Lobelia actually prefers cool temperatures and grows best in areas that receive some shade and lots of moisture. If your lobelia is grown in a larger container (so it doesn't dry out as easily) with other plants (that can provide some shade), it will tolerate more sun.

Marigold 'Safari Red'

Jim ❖ The vegetatively propagated *Lobelia ricardii* has a higher tolerance for sun and drought and will do well by itself in a hanging basket.

Can I cut back straggly lobelia?

Jim ❖ Yes. Lobelia responds well to trimming because it branches very easily and produces so many flowers. When your lobelia gets straggly, it usually means it's not getting enough water and sunlight.

Marigolds

My marigolds were in full flower when I purchased them. Will they continue to bloom all summer?

Lois ❖ Marigolds are wonderful. They're very free flowering and bloom continuously all summer, right up until freeze up. If you want lots of flowers right away, buy large, well-branched plants.

I've heard that marigolds repel insects. Is this true?

Jim ❖ Marigolds aren't particularly prone to insect attacks, but I've seen them attacked by aphids and spider mites, and I know that thrips love them. They do repel nematodes, worm-like insects which inhabit the soil in some regions. Marigolds contain toxic sulphur-containing chemicals called plythienyls that inhibit nematodes. Although the insects will penetrate marigold roots, they cannot feed or multiply. Nematodes don't exist in our region, however.

A friend of mine told me to cover my marigolds with a black cloth to stimulate them to bloom early. Will this work?

Lois ❖ Most African marigolds, such as the Atlantis series and Sweet Cream, will initiate flowering faster under short days. We cover our young transplants for a period of two weeks in the greenhouse to encourage the plants to bloom in the packs. However, for the home gardener, it is not really necesary. African marigolds bloom easily and early without extra treatment.

Jim ❖ These varieties are "facultative short-day plants," which means that they will bloom without short-day treatment, but blossoming is triggered by shorter day lengths. They will bloom more with black cloth. Professional growers typically cover them for two or three hours in the early evening, to make sure they're in the dark for at least 12.5 hours each night

My marigolds are healthy when I plant them. As the season progresses, however, the leaves turn speckled and yellow, and the plants lose their vigour. Sometimes I can see fine webs on the leaves. What might cause these symptoms?

Jim ❖ This is caused by spider mites, which can be treated with insecticidal soap.

Is there a true white marigold?

Lois ❖ The lovely "Sweet Cream" is a marigold with large (9 cm), creamy-white, double blooms.

Jim ❖ There are no true white marigolds. However, breeders continue to try to develop one, so there may be a true white marigold available in the not-too-distant future.

What are the differences between the varieties of marigolds (African vs. French, etc.)?

Lois ❖ African marigolds are tall plants that produce large (45–70 cm), round flowers in solid tones of orange, yellow, gold, and cream. French marigolds tend to be shorter (25–40 cm) with smaller flowers in a great variety of petal types, markings, bicolour combinations, and solid colours.

I've always planted marigolds, because I love their bright-yellow colour, but I want a change. Are there any other bright-yellow annual flowers that will do well in full sun?

Lois ❖ Marigolds are still a favourite of mine. If you like bright-yellow marigold flowers, remember there are now many varieties available. African types are available in primrose-yellow, lemon-yellow, and golden-yellow shades. French marigolds also offer all these shades of yellow, but with different petal types. Try the Bonanza series for crested flowers, the Safari series for anemone-like flowers, and the Disco series for single petals.

Jim ❖ There are also many other bright-yellow annuals that would be an excellent choice for full sun; don't be afraid to experiment. Check a garden centre or reliable catalogue for a wide range of suggestions.

Marigold 'Marvel Yellow'

Some Terrific Yellow Annuals

Cosmic Yellow Cosmos
Figaro Yellow Dahlias
Daybreak Yellow Gazania
Chico Yellow Helichrysum
Bingo Yellow Pansies
Madness Yellow Petunias
Sundial Yellow Portulaca
Indian Summer Rudbeckia
Ribbon Yellow
  Snapdragons
Benary Giant
  Yellow Zinnias

Nicotiana

Are all varieties of nicotiana fragrant?

Lois ❖ No, they're not. Most of the species varieties of nicotiana are fragrant, but many of the newer hybrid varieties do not have a fragrance. *Nicotiana sylvestris* is extremely fragrant, as are *N. alata*, *N. affinis*, and *N. grandiflora*.

As you probably already know, the fragrance from nicotiana is strongest in the evening. I like to plant mine near our deck so I can enjoy its wonderful perfume as I sit with a cup of tea after supper.

Is nicotiana the same as a tobacco plant?

Lois ❖ No, they're not the same plant, although they are in the same family (Solanaceae) and genus (*Nicotiana*). Although the annual flowering nicotiana has commonly been referred to as flowering tobacco, they are different species.

As I mentioned above, there are several species of flowering nicotiana, including *Nicotiana alata*, *N. affinis*, *N. grandiflora*, *N. langsdorfii*, *N. hybrida*, and *N. sylvestris*. The tobacco plant (the one that comes with the government health-warning) is the species *N. tabacum*.

Ornamental Cabbage

What is the matter with my ornamental cabbage or kale? The plant is very stunted, with small heads.

Jim ❖ There are two possibilities to consider:

• If the plants overgrow their packs before being transplanted, head formation can be prematurely triggered. When this happens, the plants remain stunted for the entire season.

• Just like their edible cousins, ornamental cabbage and kale can suffer from root maggots. The maggots tunnel deep into the roots and reduce the plant's ability to absorb water and nutrients. Drench the soil with diazinon. It's best to rotate crops like cabbage or kale to another location next year.

Are ornamental cabbages and regular cabbages the same species?

Lois ❖ No, but they are closely related. In fact, you can eat your ornamental cabbage, but as I always say, there's a difference between edible and palatable.

Jim ❖ They're not the same species, but they are the same genus—*Brassica*. The genus contains many different species, including regular cabbage, ornamental cabbage, flowering kale, Chinese cabbage, and cauliflower. Although closely related, each of these plants has its own unique characteristics.

Is ornamental cabbage susceptible to cutworms like edible cabbage?

Lois ❖ Yes.

Jim ❖ Since ornamental cabbage and edible cabbage belong to the same genus, they are attacked by many of the same pests.

Pansies

Do pansies have a fragrance?

Lois ❖ Yes, some pansies have a lovely fragrance. The most fragrant are Bingo Clear Yellow and Baby Bingo Clear Yellow. Bingo Yellow with Blotch and Bingo Clear White have a more subtle fragrance.

Will my pansies bloom all summer?

Lois ❖ Yes, they will in regions with cool summers. Pansies love cooler temperatures, performing at their best when temperatures are in the high teens and low 20s. In hotter conditions, pansies will burn out. In many areas, pansies are sold again in the fall when temperatures begin to cool. At Hole's, we sell pansies right through September.

Are pansies frost tolerant? Are some varieties hardier than others?

Jim ❖ Nothing's tougher than a pansy! Pansies are the hardiest annuals you can plant. They're the first ones we plant out in the garden in the spring, and they're the last to stop blooming in the fall. We've had our pansies outside at temperatures exceeding -10°C, and they've survived beautifully.

What's so special about the Bingo pansies you talk about, Lois?

Lois ❖ Who can resist the sight of a big batch of Bingo pansies? They really do seem to look up at you and smile! Bingos bloom early and have a bushy, compact growth habit. They also have excellent heat tolerance, especially in areas where heat can reduce flower size. They also can't be beat for really vibrant, brilliant colours. Bingo Yellow has one of the sweetest fragrances in the garden.

Jim ❖ Bingo pansies seem to "look up" because the blooms have short, strong peduncles so that the flowers face up rather than vertically.

Will pansies come back next year?

Lois ❖ In milder climates, pansies overwinter very well. In many areas of the country with milder winters, they are sold as a winter annual. In regions with colder winters, pansies will overwinter provided that there is a good, thick snow cover and temperatures aren't too cold. Although pansies will not overwinter in my area, I have a big pot of pansies on my deck from mid April through to late October.

Something's eating my pansies. The lower leaves have holes, and I can see silvery streaks near the base of my plants. Help!

Jim ❖ Those slimy trails are left behind by slugs. Slugs prefer cool, moist areas with plenty of places to hide (see the section on pests).

Petunias & Calibrachoa

One of my petunia flowers is a completely different colour than any other blossom on the same plant. Why?

Jim ❖ Sometimes the cells on a plant's growing point mutate, resulting in a different colour of flower. The shade of the flowers can also be affected by temperature. If the weather is cool when the buds are forming, the flowers will be more intensely coloured.

Why does my calibrachoa have lime-green leaves?

Lois ❖ This is usually a sign that it isn't getting enough fertilizer. Add a pinch every time you water! Calibrachoa uses a lot of fertilizer, so don't worry about giving it too much. Use a complete fertilizer, such as 20-20-20, and add some chelated iron—calibrachoa loves extra iron.

Jim ❖ That lime-green colour is almost certainly the result of an iron deficiency. Calibrachoa needs lots of iron. I've found that the white varieties have a particularly high demand for it. Although 20-20-20 and 30-10-10 contain iron, it's a good idea to add extra, as Mom suggests. Use either micronized or chelated iron. Iron filings won't work because they're not soluble.

What is a groundcover petunia?

Lois ❖ Groundcover petunia is the common name for a new type of spreading petunia. These extremely vigorous plants can spread to 1 m in just a few weeks. My favourite series is the Wave petunias. They are free-flowering all season without being cut back or deadheaded. They tolerate both hot and cold temperatures very well and have excellent weather tolerance.

My petunia flowers seem to be getting smaller. What's wrong?

Jim ❖ This is a very difficult question to answer without examining the plant. A few possibilites to consider are:

- Lack of light.
- Lack of fertilizer.
- Stress (for example the plant could be overgrown in a container that is too small, crowded by other plants, or dried out several times).
- Older varieties that don't perform as well in the garden.
- Viral disease.

I like petunias, but I'm not crazy about deadheading. I've also noticed that my petunias always look bad for several days after it rains. Are there any varieties that don't have these problems?

Lois ❖ I must admit, deadheading petunias is not my favourite job either. That's why I'm so fond of certain series. For standard petunias, the Madness series is still my favourite. It blooms consistently throughout the summer without the need to remove spent flowers. The grandiflora variety Storm is also (as its name implies) a very care-free variety. For groundcover petunias, the Waves and Tidal Waves are outstanding—again, no deadheading is necessary for a great show and masses of flowers from spring to fall. All three of these series also recover very quickly after a heavy rain.

What are the best petunias for hanging baskets?

Lois ❖ In mixed hanging baskets, my favourite petunias are the Madness series, partly because of the 21 different colours available, but you still can't beat the Wave petunias for vigour, performance, and showiness. They are also easy to maintain: all they need is regular water, fertilizer, and a sunny location.

Rudbeckia

My Indian Summer rudbeckia is so slow to bloom. What can I do to encourage it to flower earlier?

Lois ❖ Rudbeckia grows very slowly from seed, ranging from 16 to 18 weeks. We sow ours in January. If you're direct seeding rudbeckia into your garden or transplanting small plants, chances are you won't see flowers until late summer or early fall. We sell the variety Indian Summer as large plants in 21-cm (2-gallon) pots. I planted some on my deck, and they were in bloom by the late part of June and bloomed until the first frost.

Jim ❖ Rudbeckia requires long days to initiate flowering. In the greenhouse, we use supplemental light in February and March to shorten the time to flower. In more northern locations—places with long spring and early-summer days—if you purchase large plants, they should begin to flower by the late spring.

Rudbeckia 'Indian Summer'

Sweet Peas

When is the earliest I can plant sweet peas in my garden?

Lois ❖ Sweet peas are quite frost tolerant. Sow them into the garden as soon as the ground is warm enough to work! I typically plant mine in April, the first chance I can get into the garden.

Jim ❖ Go ahead and plant your sweet peas early. The sooner you plant them, the sooner you'll be enjoying them. They actually prefer cool soil temperatures for germination.

Sunflowers

Do sunflowers turn to face the sun?

Lois ❖ They certainly do. When I was growing up in Saskatchewan, it seemed as if sunflowers were planted on every farm. If you check them during the day, you'll notice that sunflowers seem to follow the sun with a wistful gaze.

Jim ❖ Sunflowers are heliotropic—that is, they follow the sun as it travels across the sky. The flowers and leaves turn to face the rising sun in the east and follow it across the sky. The genus name, *Helianthus*, is derived from the Greek words *helios* (sun) and *anthos* (flower). .

I've heard that you can eat sunflowers. Are all sunflowers edible?

Lois ❖ Everybody knows you can eat sunflower seeds, but most people are surprised to learn that you can also dine on the flower buds and petals. All varieties are edible.

Jim ❖ Edible flowers are really catching on. A lot of people who've read Mom's book *Herbs and Edible Flowers* are amazed at how many flowers you can actually eat.

Snapdragons

What is the best trailing snapdragon? What colours are available?

Lois ❖ The Lampion series of snapdragons are just beautiful with their large flowers and excellent mounding habit. They're available in six colours—apple-blossom, pink, purple, salmon orange, white and yellow. My favourite way to grow them is to mix the colours in a large hanging basket.

I've heard that I should remove the first flower stem from each snapdragon plant before it opens. Is this true?

Lois ❖ When we first grew snapdragons, we always used to pinch the first main flower stem to encourage the plants to bush. However, breeding advancements with newer varieites no longer make this necessary. The dwarf varieties require no pinching. You can still remove the first flower stem on the taller varieties, but they no longer require it.

Jim ❖ In a lot of plants, it's a good idea to pinch early, when you see the dominant stem going up. This encourages lateral buds to grow. I do recommend removing spent flower stems on snapdragons to encourage continual blooming throughout the summer season.

Snapdragon 'Lampion Purple'

Salvia

What is the difference between *Salvia splendens, Salvia farinaceae, Salvia coccinea,* and *Salvia horminum*?

Jim ❖ Although there are hundreds of species of salvia grown throughout the world, these four species are the main ones grown as bedding plants.

Salvia splendens is the most common variety and also the variety most people mean when they ask for salvia. The plants produce a profusion of large, full flower spikes, usually red, set above beautifully contrasting, deep-green foliage. They range in height from 20 to 25 cm.

Salvia farinaceae, more commonly known as mealy-cup sage, produces long, narrow flower spikes covered in tiny flowers, usually deep purple-blue, that resemble the flowers of the herb lavender. I think this is one of the most underrated annuals. It is vigorous, easy to grow, weather tolerant, and it blooms from spring until fall with virtually no care. Plants range in height from 40 to 60 cm. Mix it in a bed with bright-yellow marigolds. The results are stunning!

Salvia coccinea is a poorly know bedding salvia. It is native to Texas, and although it is a tender perennial there, it is usually grown as an annual. The plants have deep-green, heart-shaped, aromatic leaves and produce long spikes of tubular scarlet flowers, arranged in a series of rosettes along the stem. The flowers are not as abundant as on *Salvia splendens,* but the flower colour is much more intense. Plant height is 30 to 40 cm. This species is well used in borders or in your flowerbed. It also makes an unusual cutflower.

Salvia horminum, also know as clary sage, is probably the least well known of these species. The flowers are very unusual. The plants produce long, thick spikes bearing flat, widely spaced petals in soft pastel shades of cream, pink, and purple. The plants range from 45 to 50 cm in height. Although they may not be much to look at individually, they are really pretty used in bouquets with other cutflowers. I guarantee that if these are mixed in a vase on your table, everyone who sees them will ask what they are.

Statice

What is the difference between *suworoii* statice and *sinuata* statice?

Jim ❖ Statice is the common name for the genus *Limonium*. *Limonium suworoii*, also commonly called pink pokers or rat-tail statice, produces very unusual but attractive flowers. They are long, multi-branched, gracefully curved spikes of tiny, bright rose–pink flowers.

Limonium sinuata, also commonly called Mexican statice, is the more common species. This is the statice found at the florist and in arrangements. The flowers have thick, sturdy triangular stems whose ends are covered with clusters of single cups with papery petals—like the end of a brush. It is available in a wide range of colours, including dark and light purple, blue, pink, apricot, yellow, orange, and white.

Both make excellent cutflowers and can be preserved easily and beautifully by drying.

Stocks

My stocks produced one flower stalk and then went to seed with no more blooms to follow. Why?

Lois ❖ *Mathiola incana*, also known as double-flowering stocks or column stocks, is one of the oldest and most beautiful bedding plants. It's easy to grow, makes a wonderful cutflower, and its heady, clove-like scent has endeared it to generations of gardeners. But its breeding history has taken many turns.

Jim ❖ Much breeding work has been done with double-flowering stocks, focussing on two main areas: achieving 100% fully double flowers and creating varieties that will produce more than one flower spike. Florist and commercial field varieties are bred to be grown close together, with each plant producing a single large, fully double flower. Seedlings produced for this purpose receive a special cold treatment so that the grower can identify at an early stage which seedlings will produce double flowers. The single-flowered seedlings are discarded.

With renewed interest in column stocks as a bedding plant, breeding has focussed on different requirements. The newer species that we grow, such as the Harmony and Vintage series, are compact dwarf plants, 25 to 30 cm tall, and are more strongly branched, producing new flower spikes with up to 70% double blooms.

Regular water, fertilizer, and deadheading will encourage continous flowering.

Stocks 'Harmony Purple'

Tithonia

What is tithonia?

Lois ❖ *Tithonia rotundifolia*, commonly called Mexican sunflower, is a beautiful annual flower that is still largely unknown to many gardeners. It has bright-orange, dahlia-like flowers with golden-orange centres. It is native to Mexico and extremely heat and drought tolerant. Plant it in full sun in a warm location. Butterflies love it, and I've also heard that deer will leave it alone.

Jim ❖ Tithonia is sensitive to cool temperatures, so don't plant it out too early in the spring. Regular deadheading will promote continuous blooming.

Venidium

What is venidium?

Lois ❖ *Venidium fastuosom*, also known as monarch of the veldt, is another poorly known but very pretty annual. Its flowers resemble small sunflowers, with large dark-brown centres surrounded by rows of bright-orange, yellow, or white petals.

Jim ❖ Venidium is easy to grow, but it requires a warm, sunny location. The plants will reach about 60 cm and make an attractive border. This species also grows well in containers. Regular deadheading will promote continuous blooming.

Lysimachia 'Goldilocks'

Vines & Ivies

Will sweet potato vine climb?

Lois ❖ Sweet potato vines have a trailing growth habit, but won't naturally grow upwards on a trellis. The long individual stems can be attached to a trellis, but they require support and training to climb.

Will lotus vine bloom all summer?

Jim ❖ There are two species of lotus vines: *Lotus berthelotii* (parrot's beak) and *Lotus maculatus* (gold flash). Parrot's beak only blooms once per season, in the spring. However, the beautiful silver foliage of this plant is very attractive mixed in with other annuals. Gold flash blooms repeatedly as long as the nights aren't too warm—it loves nighttime temperatures between 4 and 10°C.

Last year my vinca vine produced beautiful sky-blue flowers. This year there are no flowers at all. Why?

Lois ❖ Vinca vine requires a long warm growing season to produce flowers. Chances are that last summer was very hot and sunny, while this summer has been cooler and cloudier.

Which annual vines are best for shade? For full sun?

Lois ❖ There are so many choices for annual vines now. Some of my favourites for sun are canary bird vine, morning glories, mandevilla and creeping Jenny (trailing). For shady locations I still love English ivy, black-eyed susan vine, and trailing nasturtiums.

Are the English ivies that you sell with the bedding plants the same varieties we grow as houseplants?

Lois ❖ Yes, they are. Although hardy varieties of English ivy grow as perennials in many regions, it is not a perennial in my area. English ivy has always been one of my favourite ivies to mix into containers because it's so reliable and is available in so many interesting varieties. There are different leaf shapes and bicolour combinations as well as the standard green.

Viola 'Sorbet Y.T.T.'

Why are the leaves on my morning glories turning yellow?

Lois ❖ This is another of those questions that is impossible to answer accurately without seeing the specimen. Chances are it could be one of two problems. If it is early in the year, cool temperatures can cause new leaves to yellow slightly. Otherwise, chances are that your plants are suffering from lack of fertilizer. Because morning glories are extremely vigourous vines, they require regular fertilizing with a good all-purpose fertilizer such as 20-20-20.

Violas

Why do the ants seem to love my violas? Are they harming them?

Jim ❖ No! Ants have a symbiotic relationship with violas and are vital in dispersing the seeds of many viola species.

Violas have developed a special adaptation on the exterior of their seeds called an *elaisome*, a fleshy appendage rich in fats, proteins, starch, sugars, and vitamins. Ants carry the seeds to their nest and use the elaisomes for food, leaving the seed intact. Ants don't harm violas, unless their nest happens to interfere with the plant's root system.

Verbena

What is the difference between vegetatively propagated verbena and verbena grown from seed?

Lois ❖ Trailing verbena is vegetatively propagated, while garden verbena is grown from seed. Both types of verbena thrive in hot, sunny locations in your garden. But here's a hint: never let your verbena plants dry out. The plants won't die, but they will stop flowering for a while.

Jim ❖ *Verbena hortensis*, or *Verbena hybrida*, is commonly known as garden verbena. It has a bushy, mounding growth habit and reaches 20 to 25 cm in height. It produces tiny flowers in large, showy clusters over the top of the plant, in colours from purple or purple-blue to scarlet, rose, carmine, pink, coral, and white. Although it grows well tucked into containers, it is generally planted in mass groups or borders in flowerbeds.

Verbena peruviana, more commonly known as Peruvian verbena, trailing verbena, or vegetative verbena, has been gaining popularity in the past few years. It went out of favour as a bedding plant many years ago because of its scrawny, sprawling growth habit and its vulnerability to insects and disease.

However, the past few years have produced some marvellous new vegetative series, including the Tapien, Temari, Aztec, and Wildfire series. These new varieties have proved to have a much-improved, bushy, trailing growth habit, increased production of brighter, larger flowers, and greater disease resistance (although powdery mildew can still be an occasional problem). Trailing verbena typically grows 40 to 50 cm and does well in containers and hanging baskets.

Xeranthemum

What is xeranthemum?

Lois ❖ *Xeranthemum annum*, commonly called paper daisy or paper flower, is an annual everlasting plant. Everlasting means that the plant remains in a near-perfect state indefinitely after drying. The rose-pink and white flowers are produced on long stems and are star-shaped, with papery petals. They make excellent cutflowers, fresh or dried. Xeranthemum flowers prolifically from early summer until frost. Plant it in a sunny location in your cutflower garden.

Zinnia

What is the difference between *Zinnia elegans, Zinnia angustifolia,* and *Zinnia linearis?*

Lois ❖ *Zinnia elegans,* or common zinnia, is the flower most people mean when they ask for zinnias. The plants produce large, showy, fully double flowers of 8 to 13 cm, ranging from cream to pink to yellow, orange, and red. The plants range in height from 25 to 90 cm; they are bushy, grow quickly, and flower from spring until frost. Common zinnias make excellent cutflowers.

Zinnia angustifolia, also known as *Z. linearis,* differs from *Z. elegans* in both flower size and growth habit. The plants have a mounding, spreading growth habit, reaching 30 to 45 cm in height, and produce single, star-shaped flowers of 5 cm, resembling daisies. This species is an excellent choice for mass plantings because of its growth habit. It tolerates heat, humidity, and drought, and performs superbly in the garden!

Zinnias can be direct seeded into the garden once the ground is warm or, for a quicker start, are available as bedding plants.

Zinnia 'Profusion Cherry'

Afterword
by Jim Hole

I love to learn. I guess that's why I've always been more interested in the mechanics of the real world than the imaginary narratives of novels or films. Don't get me wrong—I love a good story as much as the next guy, but a chance to learn about the inner workings of nature holds more appeal for me. Sometimes Mom describes me as a kind of walking gardening encyclopedia, but the truth is, as you might have guessed, a little more complex. Although my sister-in-law calls me "Mr. Science," I don't pretend to know everything. But it bugs me if someone asks me a question and I don't know the answer. More often than not, the solution isn't in my head; I have to pull out a textbook or consult a specialist. Over the years I've naturally assimilated plenty of gardening knowledge because of that inability to let a question go without a response. Putting together these books has been very fulfilling for that reason; your questions gave me plenty of opportunity to do some extra research and discover a number of things I wasn't previously aware of.

We have to remember that Mom and I didn't write this book. It was written by everyone here at Hole's, all the staff and customers over the years, all the wonderful people Mom and I have talked to and by everyone who has ever wondered why.

So Ask Us Some Questions...

We plan to update all of the Question and Answer books periodically. If you have a gardening question that's been troubling you, write to us! While we *can't* answer your inquiries individually, your question may appear in future Q&A books—along with the answer, naturally. And don't ever think that a question is "dumb" or "too simple." Odds are that any mysteries you face are shared by countless other gardeners.

Send your questions to:
Hole's Q&A Questions
101 Bellerose Drive
St. Albert, AB T8N 8N8
CANADA

You can also email us at: yourquestions@enjoygardening.com
or visit us at www.enjoygardening.com

Index

Question: *Who is Lois Hole?*

Answer ❖ The author of eight best-selling books, Lois Hole provides practical advice that's both accessible and essential. Her knowledge springs from years of hands-on experience as a gardener and greenhouse operator. She's shared that knowledge for years through her books, her popular newspaper columns, hundreds of gardening talks all over the continent, and dozens of radio and television appearances. Never afraid to get her hands dirty, Lois answers all of your gardening questions with warmth and wit.

Question: *Who is Jim Hole?*

Answer ❖ Inheriting his mother's love of horticulture, Jim Hole grew up in the garden. After spending his formative years on the Hole farm in St. Albert, Jim attended the University of Alberta, expanding his knowledge and earning a Bachelor of Science in Agriculture. Jim appears regularly on radio and television call-in shows to share what he's learned, and writes a weekly gardening column for the *Edmonton Journal*. Jim's focus is on the science behind the garden—he explains what makes plants tick with a clear and concise style, without losing sight of the beauty and wonder that makes gardening worthwhile.

Lois and Jim have worked together for years on books, newspaper articles, and gardening talks. Working with family members Ted Hole, Bill Hole, and Valerie Hole, Lois and Jim helped to create Hole's, a greenhouse and garden centre that ranks among the largest retail gardening operations in Canada. The books in the *Q&A* series mark Lois and Jim's first official collaboration.

"One last question..."

How did you make this book?

The Publication Staff ❖ Dozens of people worked on this book, each with his or her own ideas to contribute. It began with **Bill Hole** and the idea that all the questions that Hole's staff had answered over the years would make a great book. A quick conversation with publications manager **Bruce Keith** soon dragged in **Jim Hole** and **Dave Grice**. Each of them preferred a different focus, and thus the two-part Q & A format was born!

The staff collected all the questions they had on file and everything they remembered. Then they spent the summer collecting more. **Liz Grieve** was hired to do a rough sort and divided the questions up into sections which would eventually form different books. The first three choices were made and we were off.

Jim sat down with **Julia Mamolo** and they wrote the first rough answers. These were passed on to **Lois Hole** and the rest of the family for the first kick at refinement. Meanwhile, Jim hit the books and started to dig for the "science."

As the rough text began to take shape, **Scott Rollans** was brought in to help define the new series. He began to work with the text, beating the rough metal into something resembling its final form. As the information poured in and the answers were refined, the text was turned over to staff writer **Earl Woods** to polish.

Valerie Hole, our resident bedding-plant expert, worked with Dave Grice, the bedding plant manager, to make sure all the information was current and correct. At the same time, the text hit the production department, and pictures and charts were organized. Photo editor **Christina McDonald** pulled images from Hole's image library, and designer **Greg Brown** began work on the layout.

Soon all the pieces were in place and a final edit by the experts was underway. **Leslie Vermeer** came in to proof the final pages and get the text ready for the finishing touches. Then it was off to the printer to create the book you now hold in your hands.

Publication Direction ❖ Bruce Timothy Keith
Series Editor ❖ Scott Rollans
Editorial Assistant ❖ Julia Mamolo
Additional Writing ❖ Earl J. Woods
Proofing & Editorial ❖ Leslie Vermeer
Book Design and Production ❖ Gregory Brown